LEVEL 4

Jacob's Ladder

READING COMPREHENSION PROGRAM

Grades 7–9

LEVEL

4

Jacob's Ladder

READING COMPREHENSION PROGRAM

Grades 7–9

Tamra Stambaugh, Ph.D., &
Joyce VanTassel-Baska, Ed.D.

PRUFROCK PRESS INC.
WACO, TEXAS

Copyright ©2011 Prufrock Press Inc.

Edited by Jennifer Robins

Production Design by Raquel Trevino

ISBN-13: 978-1-59363-702-6

Prufrock Press Inc.
P.O. Box 8813
Waco, TX 76714-8813
Phone: (800) 998-2208
Fax: (800) 240-0333
http://www.prufrock.com

Contents

Acknowledgments

The coauthors would like to thank the following individuals: Tinsley Webster, for her creation of the biography readings, and Ashley Thomas, for her manuscript compilation and editing. Ms. Webster is a graduate student and assistant coordinator of elementary and parent education at Programs for Talented Youth, Vanderbilt University. Ms. Thomas is a graduate of Vanderbilt University and assistant coordinator at Programs for Talented Youth.

Part I: Teachers' Guide to Jacob's Ladder Reading Comprehension Program

Introduction to *Jacob's Ladder, Level 4*

Jacob's Ladder, Level 4 is a supplemental reading program that implements targeted readings from short stories, poetry, and nonfiction sources. With this program, students engage in an inquiry process that moves from lower order to higher order thinking skills. Starting with basic literary understanding, students learn to critically analyze texts by determining implications and consequences, generalizations, main ideas, and/or creative synthesis. Suggested for students in grades 7–9 to enhance reading comprehension and critical thinking, *Jacob's Ladder 4* tasks are organized into six skill ladders: A–F. Each ladder focuses on a different skill. Students "climb" each ladder by answering lower level questions before moving to higher level questions or rungs at the top of each ladder. Each ladder stands alone and focuses on a separate critical thinking component in reading.

Ladder A focuses on implications and consequences. By leading students through sequencing and cause and effect activities, they learn to draw implications and consequences from readings. Ladder B focuses on making generalizations. Students first learn to provide details and examples, and then move to classifying and organizing those details in order to make generalizations. Ladder C focuses on themes. Students begin by identifying setting and characters and then make inferences about the literary situation. Ladder D focuses on creative synthesis by leading students through paraphrasing and summarizing activities. Ladder E focuses on readers' emotional responses to the literature by understanding emotion, expressing it, and then channeling it productively. Ladder F provides an emphasis on metacognition by engaging learners in reflecting on the literature read and on their own applications of it for their lives. Table 1 provides a visual representation of the six ladders and corresponding objectives for each ladder and rung.

The *Jacob's Ladder* series consists of five levels: 1, 2, 3, 4, and 5. All five levels contain short stories, poetry, nonfiction selections including biographies, and at least two commensurate ladders for each selection, with the exception of Level 1, in which some reading selections have one ladder. *Jacob's Ladder 1* is recommended for students in grades 2–3, *Jacob's Ladder 2* is recommended for students in grades 4–5, and *Jacob's Ladder 3* is recommended for students in grades 5–6. The newest books in the series, Levels 4 and 5, are recommended for grades 7–9. However, teachers may find that they want to vary usage beyond the recommended levels, depending on student abilities. Evidence suggests that the curriculum can be successfully implemented with gifted learners as well as promising learners and advanced readers at different grade levels.

Ladder A: Focus on Implications and Consequences

The goal of Ladder A is to develop prediction and forecasting skills by encouraging students to make connections among the information provided. Starting with sequencing, students learn to recognize basic types of change that occur within a text. Through identifying cause and effect relationships, students then can judge the impact of certain events. Finally, through recognizing consequences and implications, students predict future events as logical and identify both short- and long-term consequences by judging probable outcomes based on data provided. The rungs are as follows:

- **Ladder A, Rung 1, Sequencing:** The lowest rung on the ladder, sequencing, requires students to organize a set of information in order, based on their reading (e.g., List the steps of a recipe in order).

- **Ladder A, Rung 2, Cause and Effect:** The middle rung, cause and effect, requires students to think about relationships and identify what causes certain effects and/or what effects were brought about because of certain causes (e.g., What causes a cake to rise in the oven? What effect does the addition of egg yolks have on a batter?).

TABLE 1
Goals and Objectives of *Jacob's Ladder* by Ladder and Rung

	Ladder A	Ladder B	Ladder C	Ladder D	Ladder E	Ladder F
Rung 3	**A3: Consequences and Implications** — Students will be able to predict character actions and story outcomes and make real-world forecasts.	**B3: Generalizations** — Students will be able to make general statements about a reading and/or an idea within the reading, using data to support their statements.	**C3: Theme/Concept** — Students will be able to identify a major idea or theme common throughout the text.	**D3: Creative Synthesis** — Students will be able to create something new using what they have learned from the reading and their synopses.	**E3: Using Emotion** — Students will be able to analyze how emotion affects the passage and/or the reader.	**F3: Reflecting** — Students will be able to (a) evaluate ideas and plans, (b) provide new plans of action, and (c) explain the pros/cons of a given selection.
Rung 2	**A2: Cause and Effect** — Students will be able to identify and predict relationships between character behavior and story events and their effects upon other characters or events.	**B2: Classifications** — Students will be able to categorize different aspects of the text or identify and sort categories from a list of topics or details.	**C2: Inference** — Students will be able to use textual clues to read between the lines and make judgments about specific textual events, ideas, or character analysis.	**D2: Summarizing** — Students will be able to provide a synopsis of text sections.	**E2: Expressing Emotion** — Students will be able to articulate their feelings through a variety of media (e.g., song, art, poem, story, essay, speech).	**F2: Monitoring and Assessing** — Students will be able to analyze a plan of action (including implications, consequences, and big ideas) and articulate future goals to accomplish a task.
Rung 1	**A1: Sequencing** — Students will be able to list, in order of importance or occurrence in the text, specific events or plot summaries.	**B1: Details** — Students will be able to list specific details or recall facts related to the text or generate a list of ideas about a specific topic or character.	**C1: Literary Elements** — Students will be able to identify and explain specific story elements such as character, setting, or poetic device.	**D1: Paraphrasing** — Students will be able to restate lines read using their own words.	**E1: Understanding Emotion** — Students will be able to explain how emotion and feeling are conveyed in a text and/or their personal experience.	**F1: Planning and Goal Setting** — Students will be able to explain and design an outline or plan given certain stimuli.

- **Ladder A, Rung 3, Consequences and Implications:** The highest rung on Ladder A requires students to think about both short- and long-term events that may happen as a result of an effect they have identified (e.g., What are the short- and long-term consequences of baking at home?). Students learn to draw consequences and implications from the text for application in the real world.

Ladder B: Focus on Generalizations

The goal of Ladder B is to help students develop deductive reasoning skills, moving from the concrete elements in a story to abstract ideas. Students begin by learning the importance of concrete details and how they can be organized. By the top rung, students are able to make general statements spanning a topic or concept. The rungs are as follows:

- **Ladder B, Rung 1, Details:** The lowest rung on Ladder B, details, requires students to list examples or details from what they have read and/or to list examples they know from the real world or have read about (e.g., Make a list of types of transportation. Write as many as you can think of in 2 minutes).

- **Ladder B, Rung 2, Classifications:** The middle rung of Ladder B, classifications, focuses on students' ability to categorize examples and details based on characteristics (e.g., How might we categorize the modes of transportation you identified?). This activity builds students' skills in categorization and classification.

- **Ladder B, Rung 3, Generalizations:** The highest rung on Ladder B, generalizations, requires students to use the list and categories generated at Rungs 1 and 2 to develop two to three general statements that apply to *all* of their examples (e.g., Write three statements about transportation).

Ladder C: Focus on Themes

The goal of Ladder C is to develop literary analysis skills based on an understanding of literary elements. After completing Ladder C, students state the main themes and ideas of text after identifying the setting, characters, and context of the piece. The rungs for this ladder are as follows:

- **Ladder C, Rung 1, Literary Elements:** While working on the lowest rung of Ladder C, literary elements, students identify and/

or describe the setting or situation in which the reading occurs. This rung also requires students to develop an understanding of a given character by identifying qualities he or she possesses and comparing these qualities to other characters they have encountered in their reading (e.g., In *Goldilocks and the Three Bears*, what is the situation in which Goldilocks finds herself? What qualities do you admire in Goldilocks? What qualities do you find problematic? How is she similar or different from other fairy tale characters you have encountered?).

- **Ladder C, Rung 2, Inference:** Inference serves as the middle rung of Ladder C and requires students to think through a situation in the text and come to a conclusion based on the information and clues provided (e.g., What evidence exists that Goldilocks ate the porridge? What inferences can you make about the bears' subsequent action?).

- **Ladder C, Rung 3, Theme/Concept:** The highest rung of Ladder C, theme/concept, requires students to state the central idea or theme for a reading. This exercise necessitates that the students explain an idea from the reading that best states what the text means (e.g., How would you rename the fairy tale? Why? What is the overall theme of *Goldilocks and the Three Bears*? Which morals apply to the fairy tale? Why?).

Ladder D: Focus on Creative Synthesis

The goal of Ladder D is to help students develop skills in creative synthesis in order to foster students' creation of new material based on information from the reading. It moves from the level of restating ideas to creating new ideas about a topic or concept. The rungs are as follows:

- **Ladder D, Rung 1, Paraphrasing:** The lowest rung on Ladder D is paraphrasing. This rung requires students to restate a short passage using their own words (e.g., Rewrite the following quotation in your own words: "But as soon as [the slave] came near to Androcles, he recognized his friend, and fawned upon him, and licked his hands like a friendly dog. The emperor, surprised at this, summoned Androcles to him, who told the whole story. Whereupon the slave was pardoned and freed, and the Lion let loose to his native forest.").

- **Ladder D, Rung 2, Summarizing:** Summarizing, the middle rung on Ladder D, requires students to summarize larger sections of text by selecting the most important key points within a passage (e.g., Choose one section of the story and summarize it in five sentences).

- **Ladder D, Rung 3, Creative Synthesis:** The highest rung on Ladder D requires students to create something new using what they have learned from the reading and their synopses of it (e.g., Write another fable about the main idea you identified for this fable, using characters, setting, and a plot of your choice).

Ladder E: Focus on Emotional Development

The goal of Ladder E is to help students develop skills in using their emotional intelligence in order to regulate and modulate behavior in respect to learning. It moves from students' understanding of emotion in self and others, to expressing emotion, to channeling emotion for cognitive ends. The rungs are as follows:

- **Ladder E, Rung 1, Understanding Emotion:** The lowest rung on Ladder E is understanding emotion in oneself and others. This requires students to identify emotions in characters and relate it to their own lives (e.g., What feelings does the main character portray throughout the story? How would you compare his temperament to yours?). It also requires them to recognize emotional situations and pinpoint the nature of the emotions involved and what is causing them. Many of the poetry and fiction selections are employed to engage students in the use of this ladder.

- **Ladder E, Rung 2, Expressing Emotion:** The middle rung on Ladder E, expressing emotion, asks students to express emotion in response to their reading of various selections (e.g., The main character seems to worry too much. Is worry ever beneficial? Why or why not?). They may often do this in self-selected formats, including poetry or prose. Teachers may want to substitute kinesthetic responses in the form of dance or skits that demonstrate an emotional reaction to the selections.

- **Ladder E, Rung 3, Using Emotion:** The highest rung on Ladder E, using emotion, encourages students to begin regulating emotion for specific purposes (e.g., How does worry impact your life? What steps can you take to minimize worry? Write a personal action plan). In application to poetry, prose, and biography, students need to demonstrate a clear understanding of how to use emotion effectively for accomplishing specific ends, whether through giving a speech or writing a passionate letter in defense of an idea. The deliberate incorporation of emotion in one's communication is stressed.

Ladder F: Focus on Metacognition

The goal of Ladder F is to help students in planning, monitoring, and evaluating their academic and career goals. Through readings of eminent persons, students examine the impact of various factors that inhibit or enhance personal contributions and trajectories. Then students are asked to apply the new learning to their own individual circumstances and short- and long-term goals. The rungs are as follows:

- **Ladder F, Rung 1, Planning and Goal Setting:** The lowest rung on Ladder F, planning and goal setting, requires students to consider how talented people from all walks of life have deliberately thought about how they will live their lives (e.g., Passion and perseverance are two traits of successful individuals. Describe how this passion and perseverance were evidenced in Bourke-White's life). Through biographical inquiry, students model this behavior in setting their own academic and career goals, based on assessing their interests, aptitudes, and values.

- **Ladder F, Rung 2, Monitoring and Assessing:** The middle rung on Ladder F, monitoring and assessing, requires students to think about their capacity to complete projects and to move forward with goals and outcomes (e.g., What are you passionate about? How can you use that passion for success?). Students are asked to judge the quality of their own products and to assess their own progress toward goals by setting appropriate criteria and then applying them to a situation. By analyzing what eminent individuals have done, students are able to think about the decisions made and the timing of those decisions as they impacted life outcomes.

- **Ladder F, Rung 3, Reflecting:** The highest rung on Ladder F, reflecting, engages students in reflecting on what they have learned from their study of biography and how the principles may apply to their own life planning and career development process (e.g., Write five ways you are successful and five things you need to work on to become more successful. Design a personal growth plan with realistic and achievable goals to become more successful in at least one area of your life). Students are asked to create career plans, to apply the talent development markers to their own lives, and to select the most important aspects of a life for emulation.

Process Skills

Along with the six goals addressed by the ladders, a seventh goal focusing on process skills is incorporated in the *Jacob's Ladder* curriculum. The aim of this goal is to promote learning through interaction and discussion of reading material in the classroom. After completing the ladders and following guidelines for discussion and teacher feedback, students will be able to:

- articulate their understanding of a reading passage using textual support,
- engage in proper dialogue about the meaning of a selection, and
- discuss varied ideas about the intention of a passage both orally and in writing.

Reading Genres and Selections

The reading selections include three major genres: short stories (fables, myths, short stories, and essays), poetry, and nonfiction. In Level 4, each reading within a genre has been carefully selected or tailored for student reading accessibility and interest. The stories and poems for the *Jacob's Ladder* curriculum at each grade level were chosen with three basic criteria in mind: (1) concrete to abstract development, (2) level of vocabulary, and (3) age-appropriate themes. The readings and exercises are designed to move students forward in their abstract thinking processes by promoting critical and creative thinking. The vocabulary in each reading is grade-level appropriate; however, when new or unfamiliar words are encountered, they should be covered in class before the readings and ladder questions are assigned. Themes also are appropriate to the students' ages at each grade level and were chosen to complement themes typically seen in texts for each particular level. The short stories, poetry, and nonfiction readings with corresponding ladder sets are delineated in Part II. Table 2 outlines all Level 4 readings by genre.

TABLE 2
Jacob's Ladder 4 Selections by Genre

Short Stories	Poems	Biographies
The Wolf and the Kid originally told by Aesop	*Weathers* by Thomas Hardy	Erwin Schrödinger, physicist
The Last Lesson by Alphonse Daudet	*Sonnet 73* by William Shakespeare	Margaret Bourke-White, photographer
The Mouse by H. H. Munro	*The Clod and the Pebble* by William Blake	Itzhak Perlman, violinist
The Ransom of Red Chief by O. Henry	*Hope Is the Thing With Feathers* by Emily Dickinson	Amartya Sen, economist
The Monkey's Paw by W. W. Jacobs	*Stopping by Woods on a Snowy Evening* by Robert Frost	
The Diamond Necklace by Guy de Maupassant	*The Wild Swans at Coole* by William Butler Yeats	
The Celebrated Jumping Frog of Calaveras County by Mark Twain	*Not They Who Soar* by Paul Laurence Dunbar	
The Lottery Ticket by Anton Chekhov		

Rationale

Constructing meaning of the written word is one of the earliest tasks required of students in schools. This skill occupies the central place in the curriculum at the elementary level. Yet, approaches to teaching reading comprehension often are "skill and drill," using worksheets on low-level reading material. As a result, students frequently are unable to transfer these skills from exercise pages and apply them to new, higher level reading material.

The time expended to ensure that students become autonomous and advanced readers would suggest the need for a methodology that deliberately moves students from simple to complex reading skills with grade-appropriate texts. Such a learning approach to reading skill development ensures that students can traverse easily from basic comprehension skills to higher level critical reading skills, while using the same reading stimulus to navigate this transition. Reading comprehension is enhanced by instructional scaffolding, moving students from lower order to higher order thinking, using strategies and processes to help students analyze passages (Villaume & Brabham, 2002). In addition, teachers who emphasize higher order thinking through questions and tasks such as those at the higher rungs of each ladder promote greater reading growth (Taylor, Pearson, Peterson, & Rodriguez, 2003).

Jacob's Ladder was written in response to teacher findings that students needed additional scaffolding to consistently work at higher levels of thinking in reading. This teacher insight is buttressed by findings from cognitive science that suggest that students need to have purpose and direction for discussions of text to yield meaningful learning and that scaffolding is a necessary part of enhancing critical reading behavior (Bransford, Brown, & Cocking, 2000). Similarly, Tivnan and Hemphill (2005) studied reading reform curricula in Title I schools and found that none of the reading programs studied emphasized skills beyond basic phonemic awareness, fluency, or limited comprehension. Therefore, supplementary curriculum that focuses on higher level thinking skills is needed.

The *Jacob's Ladder* program is a compilation of the instructional scaffolding and reading exercises necessary to aid students in their journey toward becoming critical readers. Students learn concept development skills through generalizing, predicting and forecasting skills through delineating implications of events, and literary analysis skills through discerning textual meaning (VanTassel-Baska & Stambaugh, 2006a). The questions and tasks for each reading are open-ended, as this type of approach to responding to literature improves performance on comprehension tests (Guthrie, Schafer, & Huang, 2001). Progressing through the hierarchy of skills also requires students to reread the text, thereby improving meta-comprehension accuracy (Rawson, Dunlosky, & Thiede, 2000).

Research Base

A quasi-experimental study was conducted using *Jacob's Ladder* as a supplementary program for grade 3–5 students in Title I schools. After receiving professional development, teachers were instructed to implement the *Jacob's Ladder* curriculum in addition to their basal reading series and guided reading groups.

Findings from this study ($N = 495$) suggest that when compared to students who used the basal reader only, students who were exposed to the *Jacob's Ladder* curriculum showed significant gains in reading comprehension and critical thinking. Likewise, students who used the curriculum showed significant and important growth on curriculum-based assessments that included determining implications/consequences, making inferences, outlining themes and generalizations, and applying creative synthesis. Students reported greater interest in reading and alluded that the curriculum made them "think harder." Teachers reported more in-depth student discussion and personal growth in their ability to ask open-ended questions in reading (Stambaugh, 2010).

Who Should Use *Jacob's Ladder*?

Although the program is targeted for gifted learners and for promising students who need more exposure to higher level thinking skills in reading, the program may be suitable for other learners as well, including those who are twice-exceptional, students from poverty, and those from different cultural backgrounds (VanTassel-Baska & Stambaugh, 2006b). The reading selections include classic and contemporary literature that has been used at various grade levels with various groups (VanTassel-Baska & Stambaugh, 2006a). The biography material is written at the sixth-grade level and should be high interest for students interested in various careers, especially if they are female or come from different cultural groups as these underrepresented groups comprise the selections of eminent people. The poetry included in Levels 1–3 of the series was written by students of comparable ages who won writing contests.

Implementation Considerations

Teachers need to consider certain issues when implementing the *Jacob's Ladder* curriculum. Because modeling, coaching, and feedback appear to enhance student growth in reading and writing (Pressley et al., 2001; Taylor, Peterson, Pearson, & Rodriquez, 2002), it is recommended that teachers review how to complete the task ladders with the entire class at least once, outlining expectations and record-keeping tasks, as well as modeling the process prior to assigning small-group or independent work. As students gain more confidence in the curriculum, the teacher should allow more independent work coupled with small-group or paired discussion, and then whole-group sharing with teacher feedback.

Completing these activities in dyads or small groups will facilitate discussions that stress collaborative reasoning, thereby fostering greater engagement and higher level thinking (Chin, Anderson, & Waggoner, 2001; Pressley et al., 2001; Taylor et al., 2002). The stories and accompanying ladder questions and activities also may be organized into a reading center in the classroom or utilized with reading groups during guided reading.

Process of *Jacob's Ladder*

The process of inquiry and feedback, as led and modeled by the teacher, is critical to the success of the program and student mastery of process skills. Teachers need to solicit multiple student responses and encourage dialogue about various perspectives and interpretations of a given text, requiring students to justify their answers with textual support and concrete examples (VanTassel-Baska & Stambaugh, 2006a, 2006b). Sample follow-up questions and prompts such as those listed below can be used by the teacher and posted in the classroom to guide student discussion.

- That's interesting; does anyone have a different idea?
- What in the story makes you say that?
- What do you think the author means by . . . ?
- What do you think are the implications or consequences of . . . ?
- Did anyone view that differently? How?
- Does anyone have a different point of view? Justify your answer.
- In the story I noticed that . . . Do you think that might have significance to the overall meaning?
- I heard someone say that they thought the poem (story) was about . . . What do you think? Justify your answer from the events of the story.
- Do you notice any key words that might be significant? Why?
- Do you notice any words that give you a mental picture? Do those words have significance? What might they symbolize?
- I agree with . . . because . . .
- I had a different idea than . . . because . . .

Grouping Students

Jacob's Ladder may be used in a number of different grouping patterns. The program should be introduced initially as a whole-group activity directed by the teacher with appropriate open-ended questions, feedback, and monitoring. After students have examined each type of ladder with teacher guidance, they should be encouraged to use the program by writing ideas independently, sharing with a partner, and then discussing the findings with a group. The dyad approach provides maximal opportunities for student discussion of the readings and collaborative decisions about the answers to questions posed. One purpose of the program is to solicit meaningful discussion of the text, which is best accomplished in small groups of students at similar reading levels (VanTassel-Baska & Little, 2011). Research continues to support instructional grouping in reading as an important part of successful implementation of a program (Rogers, 2002).

Demonstrating Growth: Pre- and Postassessments and Student Products

The pre- and postassessments included in Appendix A were designed as a diagnostic-prescriptive approach to guide program implementation of *Jacob's Ladder*. The pretest should be administered, scored, and then used to guide student instruction and the selection of readings for varied ability groups. Both the pre- and postassessment, scoring rubric, and sample exemplars for each rubric category and level are included in Appendix A along with exemplars to guide scoring.

In both the pre- and postassessments, students read a short passage and respond to the four questions. Question 1 focuses on consequences and implications (Ladder A), Question 2 on generalization, theme, and concept (Ladders B and C), Question 3 on inference (Ladder C), and Question 4 on creative synthesis (Ladder D). By analyzing each question and scored response, teachers may select the appropriate readings and ladders based on student need.

Additionally, in Levels 4 and 5 of the curriculum, a student product is required that assesses the extent to which students can create their own literary selections, using the selections in each book as models and assessing their understanding of Ladders E and F. Emphasis is placed on their ability to plan and organize a creative piece, assess its properties, and reflect on its purpose and audience. Moreover, students are asked to both express an emotion and indicate how it was used in the written piece and for what effect. An assessment rubric accompanies the task demand in each book.

Upon conclusion of the program or as a midpoint check, the posttest may be administered to compare the pretest results and to measure growth in students' responses. These pre-post results could be used as part of a student portfolio, in a parent-teacher conference, or as documentation of curriculum effectiveness and student progress. The pre- and postassessments were piloted to ensure pre-post equivalent forms reliability ($\alpha = .76$) and interrater reliability ($\alpha = .81$).

Student Reflection, Feedback, and Record Keeping

Students may use an answer sheet such as the one provided in Appendix B for each ladder to record their personal thoughts independently before discussing them with a partner. After finishing the ladders for each reading selection, a reflection page (also in Appendix B) can be provided, indicating each student's personal assessment of the work completed. Teachers also will want to check student answers as ladder segments are completed and conduct an individual or small-group consultation to ensure that students understand why their answers may be effective or ineffective. In order to analyze student responses and progress across the program, teachers need to monitor student performance, using the student answer sheets to indicate appropriate completion of tasks. Specific comments about student work also are important to promote growth and understanding of content.

Record-keeping sheets for the class are also provided in Appendix B. On these forms, teachers record student progress on a 3-point scale: 2 (*applies skills very effectively*), 1 (*understands and applies skills*), or 0 (*needs more practice with the given skill set*) across readings and ladder sets. This form can be used as part of a diagnostic-prescriptive approach to selecting reading materials and ladders based on student understanding or the need for more practice.

Sample Concluding Activities: Ideas for Grades

Grading the ladders and responses are at the teacher's discretion. Teachers should not overemphasize the lower rungs in graded activities. Lower rungs are intended only as a vehicle to the higher level questions at the top of the ladder. Instead, top-rung questions may be used as a journal prompt or as part of a graded, open-ended writing response. Grades also could be given based on guided discussion after students are trained on appropriate ways to discuss literature. Additional ideas for grading are as follows:

- Write a persuasive essay to justify what you think the story is about.
- Create a symbol to show the meaning of the story. Write two sentences to justify your symbol.

- In one word or phrase, what is this story mostly about? Justify your answer using examples from the story.

- Write a letter from the author's point of view, explaining what the meaning of the story is to young children.

- Pretend you are an illustrator and need to create a drawing for the story or poem that shows what the story or poem is mostly about. Write a sentence to describe your illustration and why it is the best option.

- You have been reading biographies of eminent people in many fields. Select one and act out a scene from the person's life as you imagine it.

- The importance of emotion in storytelling cannot be overstressed. Analyze a favorite story according to its emotional content and how it contributed to your liking the story.

Time Allotment

Although the time needed to complete *Jacob's Ladder* tasks will vary by student, most lessons should take students 15–30 minutes to read the selection and another 15–20 minutes to complete one ladder individually. More time is required for paired student and whole-group discussion of the questions. Teachers may wish to set aside 2 days each week for focusing on one *Jacob's Ladder* reading and its commensurate ladders, especially when introducing the program.

Answer Sets

Because the questions for Ladders E and F are highly individualized and open-ended, no answer sets are given in Levels 4 and 5 of the program. Also, students in grades 7–9 should be encouraged to seek out the levels of meaning in rich text, looking for multiple answers that reflect their own experience.

Alignment to Standards

Appendix C contains alignment charts to demonstrate the connection of the fiction and nonfiction reading materials to relevant national standards. One of the benefits of this program is its ability to provide cross-disciplinary coverage of standards through the use of a single reading stimulus. Connections to science and social studies standards are noted. Alignment to the new national standards in English/language arts have been used as the basis for the analysis.

References

Bransford, J. D., Brown, A. L., & Cocking, R. R. (2000). *How people learn: Brain, mind, experience.* Washington, DC: National Academy Press.

Chin, C. A., Anderson, R. C., & Waggoner, M. A. (2001). Patterns of discourse in two kinds of literature discussion. *Reading Research Quarterly, 30,* 378–411.

Guthrie, J. T., Schafer, W. D., & Huang, C. (2001). Benefits of opportunity to read and balanced instruction on the NAEP. *Journal of Educational Research, 94,* 145–162.

Pressley, M., Wharton-McDonald, R., Allington, R., Block, C. C., Morrow, L., Tracey, D., . . . Woo, D. (2001). A study of effective first-grade literacy instruction. *Scientific Studies of Reading, 5,* 35–58.

Rawson, K. A., Dunlosky, J., & Thiede, K. W. (2000). The rereading effect: Metacomprehension accuracy improves across reading trials. *Memory & Cognition, 28*(6), 1004.

Rogers, K. (2002). *Re-forming gifted education: How parents and teachers can match the program to the child.* Scottsdale, AZ: Great Potential Press.

Stambaugh, T. (2010). *Effects of the Jacob's Ladder Reading Comprehension Program.* Manuscript submitted for publication.

Taylor, B. M., Pearson, P. D., Peterson, D. S., & Rodriguez, M. C. (2003). Reading growth in high-poverty classrooms: The influence of teacher practices that encourage cognitive engagement in literacy learning. *The Elementary School Journal, 104,* 3–30.

Taylor, B. M., Peterson, D. P., Pearson, P. D., & Rodriguez, M. C. (2002). Looking inside classrooms: Reflecting on the "how" as well as the "what" in effective reading instruction. *Reading Teacher, 56,* 270–279.

Tivnan, T., & Hemphill, L. (2005). Comparing four literacy reform models in high-poverty schools: Patterns of first grade achievement. *Elementary School Journal, 105,* 419–443.

VanTassel-Baska, J., & Stambaugh, T. (2006a). *Comprehensive curriculum for gifted learners* (3rd ed.). Needham Heights, MA: Allyn & Bacon.

VanTassel-Baska, J., & Stambaugh, T. (2006b). Project Athena: A pathway to advanced literacy development for children of poverty. *Gifted Child Today, 29*(2), 58–65.

VanTassel-Baska, J., & Little, C. (Eds.). (2011). *Content-based curriculum for gifted learners* (2nd ed.). Waco, TX: Prufrock Press.

Villaume, S. K., & Brabham, E. G. (2002). Comprehension instruction: Beyond strategies. *The Reading Teacher, 55,* 672–676.

Part II: Readings and Student Ladder Sets

CHAPTER

1

Short Stories

Chapter 1 includes the selected readings and accompanying question sets for each short story selection. Each reading is followed by two or three sets of questions; each set is aligned to one of the six sets of ladder skills.

For *Jacob's Ladder 4*, the skills covered by each selection are as follows:

Name: _____   Date: _____

The Wolf and the Kid
Originally told by Aesop

A Kid was perched up on the top of a house, and looking down saw a Wolf passing under him. Immediately he began to revile and attack his enemy. "Murderer and thief," he cried, "what are you doing here near honest folks' houses? How dare you make an appearance where your vile deeds are known?"

"Curse away, my young friend," said the Wolf. "It is easy to be brave from a safe distance."

Creative Synthesis

D3

Write a present-day fable that has the same life lesson.

Summarizing

D2

Summarize the story in two sentences.

Paraphrasing

D1

In your own words explain what is meant by "It
is easy to be brave from a safe distance."

THE WOLF AND THE KID

Using Emotion

E3

What advice would you give someone who felt
like he or she was in a no-win situation?

Expressing Emotion

E2

What steps can you take to become less wolf- or kid-like? List them.

Understanding Emotion

E1

Are you more like the wolf or the kid in real life?

THE WOLF AND THE KID

The Last Lesson
by Alphonse Daudet

I started for school very late that morning and was in great dread of a scolding, especially because M. Hamel had said that he would question us on participles, and I did not know the first word about them. For a moment I thought of running away and spending the day out of doors. It was so warm, so bright! The birds were chirping at the edge of the woods; and in the open field back of the sawmill the Prussian soldiers were drilling. It was all much more tempting than the rule for participles, but I had the strength to resist, and hurried off to school.

When I passed the town hall there was a crowd in front of the bulletin-board. For the last two years all our bad news had come from there—the lost battles, the draft, the orders of the commanding officer—and I thought to myself, without stopping:

"What can be the matter now?"

Then, as I hurried by as fast as I could go, the blacksmith, Wachter, who was there, with his apprentice, reading the bulletin, called after me:

"Don't go so fast, bub; you'll get to your school in plenty of time!"

I thought he was making fun of me, and reached M. Hamel's little garden all out of breath.

Usually, when school began, there was a great bustle, which could be heard out in the street, the opening and closing of desks, lessons repeated in unison, very loud, with our hands over our ears to understand better, and the teacher's great ruler rapping on the table. But now it was all so still! I had counted on the commotion to get to my desk without being seen; but, of course, that day everything had to be as quiet as Sunday morning. Through the window I saw my classmates, already in their places, and M. Hamel walking up and down with his terrible iron ruler under his arm. I had to open the door and go in before everybody. You can imagine how I blushed and how frightened I was.

But nothing happened. M. Hamel saw me and said very kindly:

"Go to your place quickly, little Franz. We were beginning without you."

I jumped over the bench and sat down at my desk. Not till then, when I had got a little over my fright, did I see that our teacher had on his beautiful green coat, his frilled shirt, and the little black silk cap, all embroidered,

that he never wore except on inspection and prize days. Besides, the whole school seemed so strange and solemn. But the thing that surprised me most was to see, on the back benches that were always empty, the village people sitting quietly like ourselves; old Hauser, with his three-cornered hat, the former mayor, the former postmaster, and several others besides. Everybody looked sad; and Hauser had brought an old primer, thumbed at the edges, and he held it open on his knees with his great spectacles lying across the pages.

While I was wondering about it all, M. Hamel mounted his chair, and, in the same grave and gentle tone which he had used to me, said:

"My children, this is the last lesson I shall give you. The order has come from Berlin to teach only German in the schools of Alsace and Lorraine. The new master comes to-morrow. This is your last French lesson. I want you to be very attentive."

What a thunderclap these words were to me!

Oh, the wretches; that was what they had put up at the town-hall!

My last French lesson! Why, I hardly knew how to write! I should never learn any more! I must stop there, then! Oh, how sorry I was for not learning my lessons, for seeking birds' eggs, or going sliding on the Saar! My books, that had seemed such a nuisance a while ago, so heavy to carry, my grammar, and my history of the saints, were old friends now that I couldn't give up. And M. Hamel, too; the idea that he was going away, that I should never see him again, made me forget all about his ruler and how cranky he was.

Poor man! It was in honor of this last lesson that he had put on his fine Sunday clothes, and now I understood why the old men of the village were sitting there in the back of the room. It was because they were sorry, too, that they had not gone to school more. It was their way of thanking our master for his forty years of faithful service and of showing their respect for the country that was theirs no more.

While I was thinking of all this, I heard my name called. It was my turn to recite. What would I not have given to be able to say that dreadful rule for the participle all through, very loud and clear, and without one mistake? But I got mixed up on the first words and stood there, holding on to my desk, my heart beating, and not daring to look up. I heard M. Hamel say to me:

"I won't scold you, little Franz; you must feel bad enough. See how it is! Every day we have said to ourselves: 'Bah! I've plenty of time. I'll learn it to-morrow.' And now you see where we've come out. Ah, that's the great trouble with Alsace; she puts off learning till to-morrow. Now those fellows out there will have the right to say to you: 'How is it; you pretend to be Frenchmen, and yet you can neither speak nor write your own language?' But you are not the worst, poor little Franz. We've all a great deal to reproach ourselves with.

"Your parents were not anxious enough to have you learn. They preferred to put you to work on a farm or at the mills, so as to have a little more money. And I? I've been to blame also. Have I not often sent you to water my flowers instead of learning your lessons? And when I wanted to go fishing, did I not just give you a holiday?"

Then, from one thing to another, M. Hamel went on to talk of the French language, saying that it was the most beautiful language in the world—the clearest, the most logical; that we must guard it among us and never forget it, because when a people are enslaved, as long as they hold fast to their language it is as if they had the key to their prison. Then he opened a grammar and read us our lesson. I was amazed to see how well I understood it. All he said seemed so easy, so easy! I think, too, that I had never listened so carefully, and that he had never explained everything with so much patience. It seemed almost as if the poor man wanted to give us all he knew before going away, and to put it all into our heads at one stroke.

After the grammar, we had a lesson in writing. That day M. Hamel had new copies for us, written in a beautiful round hand: France, Alsace, France, Alsace. They looked like little flags floating everywhere in the school-room, hung from the rod at the top of our desks. You ought to have seen how every one set to work, and how quiet it was! The only sound was the scratching of the pens over the paper. Once some beetles flew in; but nobody paid any attention to them, not even the littlest ones, who worked right on tracing their fish-hooks, as if that was French, too. On the roof the pigeons cooed very low, and I thought to myself:

"Will they make them sing in German, even the pigeons?"

Whenever I looked up from my writing I saw M. Hamel sitting motionless in his chair and gazing first at one thing, then at another, as if he wanted to fix in his mind just how everything looked in that little school-room. Fancy! For forty years he had been there in the same place, with his garden outside the window and his class in front of him, just like that. Only the desks and benches had been worn smooth; the walnut-trees in the garden were taller, and the hopvine that he had planted himself twined about the windows to the roof. How it must have broken his heart to leave it all, poor man; to hear his sister moving about in the room above, packing their trunks! For they must leave the country next day.

But he had the courage to hear every lesson to the very last. After the writing, we had a lesson in history, and then the babies chanted their ba, be, bi, bo, bu. Down there at the back of the room old Hauser had put on his spectacles and, holding his primer in both hands, spelled the letters with them. You could see that he, too, was crying; his voice trembled with emotion, and it was so funny to hear him that we all wanted to laugh and cry. Ah, how well I remember it, that last lesson!

All at once the church-clock struck 12. Then the Angelus. At the same moment the trumpets of the Prussians, returning from drill, sounded under our windows. M. Hamel stood up, very pale, in his chair. I never saw him look so tall.

"My friends," said he, "I—I—" But something choked him. He could not go on.

Then he turned to the blackboard, took a piece of chalk, and, bearing on with all his might, he wrote as large as he could:

"Vive La France!"

Then he stopped and leaned his head against the wall, and, without a word, he made a gesture to us with his hand:

"School is dismissed—you may go."

Consequences and Implications

A3

What are the implications of culture on literary works in general? Defend your answer using examples from this story and others you have read.

Cause and Effect

A2

What effects did the culture of the day have on the author? How did he portray this in his writing?

Sequencing

A1

Find out more about the French and Prussian war. Sequence the events of the war and its impact on each side.

THE LAST LESSON

Theme/Concept

C3

What is the central theme Daudet is trying
to convey? Defend your answer.

Inference

C2

What is the significance of the French lesson on the
meaning of the story? Why didn't the author use
another subject such as history or math?

Literary Elements

C1

Why do you think Daudet chose to convey his story
through the point of view of a young boy?

THE LAST LESSON

THE LAST LESSON

Reflecting

F3

Does the writer shape the culture or does the culture shape the writer? Defend your answer.

Monitoring and Assessing

F2

Consider a major event that has occurred in the U.S. during your lifetime. Write a short story from the point of view of an ordinary person to make sense of the event. Compare your story to Daudet's.

Planning and Goal Setting

F1

Which literary elements are most prevalent in conveying emotion in the story?

The Mouse

by H. H. Munro

Theodoric Voler had been brought up, from infancy to the confines of middle age, by a fond mother whose chief solicitude had been to keep him screened from what she called the coarser realities of life. When she died she left Theodoric alone in a world that was as real as ever, and a good deal coarser than he considered it had any need to be. To a man of his temperament and upbringing even a simple railway journey was crammed with petty annoyances and minor discords, and as he settled himself down in a second class compartment one September morning he was conscious of ruffled feelings and general mental discomposure. He had been staying at a country vicarage, the inmates of which had been certainly neither brutal nor bacchanalian, but their supervision of the domestic establishment had been of that lax order which invites disaster. The pony carriage that was to take him to the station had never been properly ordered, and when the moment for his departure drew near the handy-man who should have produced the required article was nowhere to be found. In this emergency Theodoric, to his mute but very intense disgust, found himself obliged to collaborate with the vicar's daughter in the task of harnessing the pony, which necessitated groping about in an ill-lighted outhouse called a stable, and smelling very like one—except in patches where it smelt of mice. Without being actually afraid of mice, Theodoric classed them among the coarser incidents of life, and considered that Providence, with a little exercise of moral courage, might long ago have recognised that they were not indispensable, and have withdrawn them from circulation. As the train glided out of the station Theodoric's nervous imagination accused himself of exhaling a weak odour of stable-yard, and possibly of displaying a mouldy straw or two on his usually well-brushed garments. Fortunately the only other occupant of the compartment, a lady of about the same age as himself, seemed inclined for slumber rather than scrutiny; the train was not due to stop till the terminus was reached, in about an hour's time, and the carriage was of the old-fashioned sort, that held no communication with a corridor, therefore no further travelling companions were likely to intrude on Theodoric's semi-privacy. And yet the train had scarcely attained its normal speed before he became reluctantly but vividly aware that he was not alone with the slumbering lady; he was not even alone in his own clothes. A warm, creeping movement over his flesh betrayed the unwelcome and highly resented presence, unseen but poignant, of a strayed mouse, that had evidently dashed into its present retreat during the episode of the pony harnessing. Furtive stamps and shakes and wildly directed pinches failed to dislodge the intruder, whose motto, indeed, seemed to be Excelsior; and the lawful occupant of the clothes lay back against the cushions and endeavoured rapidly to evolve some means for putting an end to the dual ownership. It was unthinkable that he should continue for the space of a whole hour in the horrible position of a Rowton House for vagrant mice (already his imagination had at least doubled the numbers of the alien invasion). On the other hand, nothing less drastic than partial disrobing would ease him of his tormentor, and to undress in the presence of a lady, even for so laudable a purpose, was an idea that made his eartips tingle in a blush of abject shame. He had never been able to bring himself even to the mild exposure of open-work socks in the presence of the fair sex. And yet—the lady in this case was to all appearances soundly and securely asleep; the mouse, on the other hand, seemed to be trying to crowd a Wanderjahr into a few strenuous minutes. If there is any truth in the theory of transmigration, this particular mouse must certainly have been in a former state a member of the Alpine Club. Sometimes in its eagerness it lost its footing and slipped for half an inch or so; and then, in fright, or more probably temper, it bit. Theodoric was goaded into the most audacious undertaking of his life. Crimsoning to the hue of a beetroot and keeping an agonised watch on his slumbering fellow-traveller, he swiftly and noiselessly secured the ends of his railway-rug to the racks on either side of the carriage, so that a substantial curtain hung athwart the compartment. In the narrow dressing-room that he had thus improvised he proceeded with violent haste to extricate himself partially and the mouse entirely from the surrounding casings of tweed and halfwool. As the unravelled mouse gave a wild leap to the floor, the rug, slipping its fastening at either end, also came down with a heart-curdling flop, and almost simultaneously the awakened sleeper opened her eyes. With a movement almost quicker than the mouse's, Theodoric pounced on the rug, and hauled its ample folds chin-high over his dismantled person as he collapsed into the further corner of the carriage. The blood raced and beat in the veins of his neck and forehead, while he waited dumbly for the communication-cord to be pulled. The lady, however, contented herself with a silent stare at her strangely muffled companion. How much had she seen, Theodoric queried to himself, and in any case what on earth must she think of his present posture?

"I think I have caught a chill," he ventured desperately.

"Really, I'm sorry," she replied. "I was just going to ask you if you would open this window."

"I fancy it's malaria," he added, his teeth chattering slightly, as much from fright as from a desire to support his theory.

"I've got some brandy in my hold-all, if you'll kindly reach it down for me," said his companion.

"Not for worlds—I mean, I never take anything for it," he assured her earnestly.

"I suppose you caught it in the Tropics?"

Theodoric, whose acquaintance with the Tropics was limited to an annual present of a chest of tea from an uncle in Ceylon, felt that even the malaria was slipping from him. Would it be possible, he wondered, to disclose the real state of affairs to her in small installments?

"Are you afraid of mice?" he ventured, growing, if possible, more scarlet in the face.

"Not unless they came in quantities, like those that ate up Bishop Hatto. Why do you ask?"

"I had one crawling inside my clothes just now," said Theodoric in a voice that hardly seemed his own. "It was a most awkward situation."

"It must have been, if you wear your clothes at all tight," she observed; "but mice have strange ideas of comfort."

"I had to get rid of it while you were asleep," he continued; then, with a gulp, he added, "it was getting rid of it that brought me to—to this."

"Surely leaving off one small mouse wouldn't bring on a chill," she exclaimed, with a levity that Theodoric accounted abominable.

Evidently she had detected something of his predicament, and was enjoying his confusion. All the blood in his body seemed to have mobilised in one concentrated blush, and an agony of abasement, worse than a myriad mice, crept up and down over his soul. And then, as reflection began to assert itself, sheer terror took the place of humiliation. With every minute that passed the train was rushing nearer to the crowded and bustling terminus where dozens of prying eyes would be exchanged for the one paralysing pair that watched him from the further corner of the carriage. There was one slender despairing chance, which the next few minutes must decide. His fellow-traveller might relapse into a blessed slumber. But as the minutes throbbed by that chance ebbed away. The furtive glance which Theodoric stole at her from time to time disclosed only an unwinking wakefulness.

"I think we must be getting near now," she presently observed.

Theodoric had already noted with growing terror the recurring stacks of small, ugly dwellings that heralded the journey's end. The words acted as a signal. Like a hunted beast breaking cover and dashing madly towards some other haven of momentary safety he threw aside his rug, and struggled frantically into his dishevelled garments. He was conscious of dull suburban stations racing past the window, of a choking, hammering sensation in his throat and heart, and of an icy silence in that corner towards which he dared not look. Then as he sank back in his seat, clothed and almost delirious, the train slowed down to a final crawl, and the woman spoke.

"Would you be so kind," she asked, "as to get me a porter to put me into a cab? It's a shame to trouble you when you're feeling unwell, but being blind makes one so helpless at a railway station."

Consequences and Implications

A3

What are the implications of the setting of
the story on the overall meaning?

Cause and Effect

A2

What effect did the setting have on the story?

Sequencing

A1

Sequence the top six events in the story. Justify
why those events are most important.

THE MOUSE

Theme/Concept

C3

Write a moral for this story.

Inference

C2

Why do you think the author included a blind woman as a secondary character? How does that impact the meaning of this story?

Literary Elements

C1

Explain how symbolism was used in the story. Cite specific examples.

THE MOUSE

Using Emotion

E3

How does worry impact your life? What steps can you take to minimize worry? Write a personal action plan.

Expressing Emotion

E2

The main character seems to worry too much. Is worry ever beneficial? Why or why not?

Understanding Emotion

E1

What feelings does the main character portray throughout the story? How would you compare his temperament to yours?

THE MOUSE

Name: _____   Date: _____

The Ransom of Red Chief
by O. Henry

IT LOOKED like a good thing: but wait till I tell you. We were down South, in Alabama—Bill Driscoll and myself—when this kidnapping idea struck us. It was, as Bill afterward expressed it, "during a moment of temporary mental apparition"; but we didn't find that out till later.

There was a town down there, as flat as a flannel-cake, and called Summit, of course. It contained inhabitants of as undeleterious and self-satisfied a class of peasantry as ever clustered around a Maypole.

Bill and me had a joint capital of about six hundred dollars, and we needed just two thousand dollars more to pull off a fraudulent town-lot scheme in Western Illinois with. We talked it over on the front steps of the hotel. Philoprogenitiveness, says we, is strong in semi-rural communities; therefore and for other reasons, a kidnapping project ought to do better there than in the radius of newspapers that send reporters out in plain clothes to stir up talk about such things. We knew that Summit couldn't get after us with anything stronger than constables and maybe some lackadaisical bloodhounds and a diatribe or two in the Weekly Farmers' Budget. So, it looked good.

We selected for our victim the only child of a prominent citizen named Ebenezer Dorset. The father was respectable and tight, a mortgage fancier and a stern, upright collection-plate passer and forecloser. The kid was a boy of ten, with bas-relief freckles, and hair the colour of the cover of the magazine you buy at the news-stand when you want to catch a train. Bill and me figured that Ebenezer would melt down for a ransom of two thousand dollars to a cent. But wait till I tell you.

About two miles from Summit was a little mountain, covered with a dense cedar brake. On the rear elevation of this mountain was a cave. There we stored provisions. One evening after sundown, we drove in a buggy past old Dorset's house. The kid was in the street, throwing rocks at a kitten on the opposite fence.

"Hey, little boy!" says Bill, "would you like to have a bag of candy and a nice ride?"

The boy catches Bill neatly in the eye with a piece of brick.

"That will cost the old man an extra five hundred dollars," says Bill, climbing over the wheel.

That boy put up a fight like a welter-weight cinnamon bear; but, at last, we got him down in the bottom of the buggy and drove away. We took him up to

the cave and I hitched the horse in the cedar brake. After dark I drove the buggy to the little village, three miles away, where we had hired it, and walked back to the mountain.

Bill was pasting court-plaster over the scratches and bruises on his features. There was a burning behind the big rock at the entrance of the cave, and the boy was watching a pot of boiling coffee, with two buzzard tailfeathers stuck in his red hair. He points a stick at me when I come up, and says:

"Ha! cursed paleface, do you dare to enter the camp of Red Chief, the terror of the plains?"

"He's all right now," says Bill, rolling up his trousers and examining some bruises on his shins. "We're playing Indian. We're making Buffalo Bill's show look like magic-lantern views of Palestine in the town hall. I'm Old Hank, the Trapper, Red Chief's captive, and I'm to be scalped at daybreak. By Geronimo! that kid can kick hard."

Yes, sir, that boy seemed to be having the time of his life. The fun of camping out in a cave had made him forget that he was a captive, himself. He immediately christened me Snake-eye, the Spy, and announced that, when his braves returned from the warpath, I was to be broiled at the stake at the rising of the sun.

Then we had supper; and he filled his mouth full of bacon and bread and gravy, and began to talk. He made a during-dinner speech something like this:

"I like this fine. I never camped out before; but I had a pet 'possum once, and I was nine last birthday. I hate to go to school. Rats ate up sixteen of Jimmy Talbot's aunt's speckled hen's eggs. Are there any real Indians in these woods? I want some more gravy. Does the trees moving make the wind blow? We had five puppies. What makes your nose so red, Hank? My father has lots of money. Are the stars hot? I whipped Ed Walker twice, Saturday. I don't like girls. You dassent catch toads unless with a string. Do oxen make any noise? Why are oranges round? Have you got beds to sleep on in this cave? Amos Murray has got six toes. A parrot can talk, but a monkey or a fish can't. How many does it take to make twelve?"

Every few minutes he would remember that he was a pesky redskin, and pick up his stick rifle and tiptoe to the mouth of the cave to rubber for the scouts of the hated paleface. Now and then he would let out a war-whoop that made Old Hank the Trapper shiver. That boy had Bill terrorized from the start.

"Red Chief," says I to the kid, "would you like to go home?"

"Aw, what for?" says he. "I don't have any fun at home. I hate to go to school. I like to camp out. You won't take me back home again, Snake-eye, will you?"

"Not right away," says I. "We'll stay here in the cave a while."

"All right!" says he. "That'll be fine. I never had such fun in all my life."

We went to bed about eleven o'clock. We spread down some wide blankets and quilts and put Red Chief between us. We weren't afraid he'd run away. He kept us awake for three hours, jumping up and reaching for his rifle and screeching: "Hist! pard," in mine and Bill's ears, as the fancied crackle of a twig or the rustle of a leaf revealed to his young imagination the stealthy approach of the outlaw band. At last, I fell into a troubled sleep, and dreamed that I had been kidnapped and chained to a tree by a ferocious pirate with red hair.

Just at daybreak, I was awakened by a series of awful screams from Bill. They weren't yells, or howls, or shouts, or whoops, or yalps, such as you'd expect from a manly set of vocal organs—they were simply indecent, terrifying, humiliating screams, such as women emit when they see ghosts or caterpillars. It's an awful thing to hear a strong, desperate, fat man scream incontinently in a cave at daybreak.

I jumped up to see what the matter was. Red Chief was sitting on Bill's chest, with one hand twined in Bill's hair. In the other he had the sharp case-knife we used for slicing bacon; and he was industriously and realistically trying to take Bill's scalp, according to the sentence that had been pronounced upon him the evening before.

I got the knife away from the kid and made him lie down again. But, from that moment, Bill's spirit was broken. He laid down on his side of the bed, but he never closed an eye again in sleep as long as that boy was with us. I dozed off for a while, but along toward sun-up I remembered that Red Chief had said I was to be burned at the stake at the rising of the sun. I wasn't nervous or afraid; but I sat up and lit my pipe and leaned against a rock.

"What you getting up so soon for, Sam?" asked Bill.

"Me?" says I. "Oh, I got a kind of a pain in my shoulder. I thought sitting up would rest it."

"You're a liar!" says Bill. "You're afraid. You was to be burned at sunrise, and you was afraid he'd do it. And he would, too, if he could find a match. Ain't it awful, Sam? Do you think anybody will pay out money to get a little imp like that back home?"

"Sure," said I. "A rowdy kid like that is just the kind that parents dote on. Now, you and the Chief get up and cook breakfast, while I go up on the top of this mountain and reconnoitre."

I went up on the peak of the little mountain and ran my eye over the contiguous vicinity. Over toward Summit I expected to see the sturdy yeomanry of the village armed with scythes and pitchforks beating the countryside for the dastardly kidnappers. But what I saw was a peaceful landscape dotted with one man ploughing with a dun mule. Nobody was dragging the creek; no couriers dashed hither and yon, bringing tidings of no news to the distracted parents. There was a sylvan attitude of somnolent sleepiness pervading that section of the external outward surface of Alabama that lay exposed to my view. "Perhaps," says I to myself, "it has not yet been discovered that the wolves have home away the tender lambkin from the fold. Heaven help the wolves!" says I, and I went down the mountain to breakfast.

When I got to the cave I found Bill backed up against the side of it, breathing hard, and the boy threatening to smash him with a rock half as big as a cocoanut.

"He put a red-hot boiled potato down my back," explained Bill, "and then mashed it with his foot; and I boxed his ears. Have you got a gun about you, Sam?"

I took the rock away from the boy and kind of patched up the argument. "I'll fix you," says the kid to Bill. "No man ever yet struck the Red Chief but what he got paid for it. You better beware!"

After breakfast the kid takes a piece of leather with strings wrapped around it out of his pocket and goes outside the cave unwinding it.

"What's he up to now?" says Bill, anxiously. "You don't think he'll run away, do you, Sam?"

"No fear of it," says I. "He don't seem to be much of a home body. But we've got to fix up some plan about the ransom. There don't seem to be much excitement around Summit on account of his disappearance; but maybe they haven't realized yet that he's gone. His folks may think he's spending the night with Aunt Jane or one of the neighbours. Anyhow, he'll be missed to-day. To-night we must get a message to his father demanding the two thousand dollars for his return."

Just then we heard a kind of war-whoop, such as David might have emitted when he knocked out the champion Goliath. It was a sling that Red Chief had pulled out of his pocket, and he was whirling it around his head.

I dodged, and heard a heavy thud and a kind of a sigh from Bill, like a horse gives out when you take his saddle off. A niggerhead rock the size of an egg had caught Bill just behind his left ear. He loosened himself all over and fell in the fire across the frying pan of hot water for washing the dishes. I dragged him out and poured cold water on his head for half an hour.

By and by, Bill sits up and feels behind his ear and says: "Sam, do you know who my favourite Biblical character is?"

"Take it easy," says I. "You'll come to your senses presently."

"King Herod," says he. "You won't go away and leave me here alone, will you, Sam?"

I went out and caught that boy and shook him until his freckles rattled.

"If you don't behave," says I, "I'll take you straight home. Now, are you going to be good, or not?"

"I was only funning," says he sullenly. "I didn't mean to hurt Old Hank. But what did he hit me for? I'll behave, Snake-eye, if you won't send me home, and if you'll let me play the Black Scout to-day."

"I don't know the game," says I. "That's for you and Mr. Bill to decide. He's your playmate for the day. I'm going away for a while, on business. Now, you come in and make friends with him and say you are sorry for hurting him, or home you go, at once."

I made him and Bill shake hands, and then I took Bill aside and told him I was going to Poplar Cove, a little village three miles from the cave, and find out what I could about how the kidnapping had been regarded in Summit. Also, I thought it best to send a peremptory letter to old man Dorset that day, demanding the ransom and dictating how it should be paid.

"You know, Sam," says Bill, "I've stood by you without batting an eye in earthquakes, fire and flood—in poker games, dynamite outrages, police raids, train robberies and cyclones. I never lost my nerve yet till we kidnapped that two-legged skyrocket of a kid. He's got me going. You won't leave me long with him, will you, Sam?"

"I'll be back some time this afternoon," says I. "You must keep the boy amused and quiet till I return. And now we'll write the letter to old Dorset."

Bill and I got paper and pencil and worked on the letter while Red Chief, with a blanket wrapped around him, strutted up and down, guarding the mouth of the cave. Bill begged me tearfully to make the ransom fifteen hundred dollars instead of two thousand. "I ain't attempting," says he, "to decry the celebrated moral aspect of parental affection, but we're dealing with humans, and it ain't human for anybody to give up two thousand dollars for that forty-pound chunk of freckled wildcat. I'm willing to take a chance at fifteen hundred dollars. You can charge the difference up to me."

So, to relieve Bill, I acceded, and we collaborated a letter that ran this way:

Ebenezer Dorset, Esq.:

We have your boy concealed in a place far from Summit. It is useless for you or the most skilful detectives to attempt to find him. Absolutely, the only terms on which you can have him restored to you are these: We demand fifteen hundred dollars in large bills for his return; the money to be left at midnight to-night at the same spot and in the same box as your reply—as hereinafter described. If you agree to these terms, send your answer in writing by a solitary messenger to-night at half-past eight o'clock. After crossing Owl Creek, on the road to Poplar Cove, there are three large trees about a hundred yards apart, close to the fence of the wheat field on the right-hand side. At the bottom of the fence-post, opposite the third tree, will be found a small pasteboard box. The messenger will place the answer in this box and return immediately to Summit.

If you attempt any treachery or fail to comply with our demand as stated, you will never see your boy again.

If you pay the money as demanded, he will be returned to you safe and well within three hours. These terms are final, and if you do not accede to them no further communication will be attempted.

TWO DESPERATE MEN.

I addressed this letter to Dorset, and put it in my pocket. As I was about to start, the kid comes up to me and says:

"Aw, Snake-eye, you said I could play the Black Scout while you was gone."

"Play it, of course," says I. "Mr. Bill will play with you. What kind of a game is it?"

"I'm the Black Scout," says Red Chief, "and I have to ride to the stockade to warn the settlers that the Indians are coming. I'm tired of playing Indian myself. I want to be the Black Scout."

"All right," says I. "It sounds harmless to me. I guess Mr. Bill will help you foil the pesky savages."

"What am I to do?" asks Bill, looking at the kid suspiciously.

"You are the hoss," says Black Scout. "Get down on your hands and knees. How can I ride to the stockade without a hoss?"

"You'd better keep him interested," said I, "till we get the scheme going. Loosen up."

Bill gets down on his all fours, and a look comes in his eye like a rabbit's when you catch it in a trap.

"How far is it to the stockade, kid?" he asks, in a husky manner of voice.

"Ninety miles," says the Black Scout. "And you have to hump yourself to get there on time. Whoa, now!"

The Black Scout jumps on Bill's back and digs his heels in his side.

"For Heaven's sake," says Bill, "hurry back, Sam, as soon as you can. I wish we hadn't made the ransom more than a thousand. Say, you quit kicking me or I'll get up and warm you good."

I walked over to Poplar Cove and sat around the post-office and store, talking with the chawbacons that came in to trade. One whiskerando says that he hears Summit is all upset on account of Elder Ebenezer Dorset's boy having been lost or stolen. That was all I wanted to know. I bought some smoking tobacco, referred casually to the price of black-eyed peas, posted my letter surreptitiously and came away. The postmaster said the mail-carrier would come by in an hour to take the mail on to Summit.

When I got back to the cave Bill and the boy were not to be found. I explored the vicinity of the cave, and risked a yodel or two, but there was no response.

So I lighted my pipe and sat down on a mossy bank to await developments.

In about half an hour I heard the bushes rustle, and Bill wabbled out into the little glade in front of the cave. Behind him was the kid, stepping softly like a scout, with a broad grin on his face. Bill stopped, took off his hat and wiped his face with a red handkerchief. The kid stopped about eight feet behind him.

"Sam," says Bill, "I suppose you'll think I'm a renegade, but I couldn't help it. I'm a grown person with masculine proclivities and habits of self-defense, but there is a time when all systems of egotism and predominance fail. The boy is gone. I have sent him home. All is off. There was martyrs in old times," goes on Bill, "that suffered death rather than give up the particular graft they enjoyed. None of 'em ever was subjugated to such supernatural tortures as I have been. I tried to be faithful to our articles of depredation; but there came a limit."

"What's the trouble, Bill?" I asks him.

"I was rode," says Bill, "the ninety miles to the stockade, not barring an inch. Then, when the settlers was rescued, I was given oats. Sand ain't a palatable substitute. And then, for an hour I had to try to explain to him why there was nothin' in holes, how a road can run both ways and what makes the grass green. I tell you, Sam, a human can only stand so much. I takes him by the neck of his clothes and drags him down the mountain. On the way he kicks my legs black-and-blue from the knees down; and I've got to have two or three bites on my thumb and hand cauterized.

"But he's gone"—continues Bill—"gone home. I showed him the road to Summit and kicked him about eight feet nearer there at one kick. I'm sorry we lose the ransom; but it was either that or Bill Driscoll to the madhouse."

Bill is puffing and blowing, but there is a look of ineffable peace and growing content on his rose-pink features.

"Bill," says I, "there isn't any heart disease in your family, is there?"

"No," says Bill, "nothing chronic except malaria and accidents. Why?"

"Then you might turn around," says I, "and have a took behind you."

Bill turns and sees the boy, and loses his complexion and sits down plump on the round and begins to pluck aimlessly at grass and little sticks. For an hour I was afraid for his mind. And then I told him that my scheme was to put the whole job through immediately and that we would get the ransom and be off with it by midnight if old Dorset fell in with our proposition. So Bill braced up enough to give the kid a weak sort of a smile and a promise to play the Russian in a Japanese war with him as soon as he felt a little better.

I had a scheme for collecting that ransom without danger of being caught by counterplots that ought to commend itself to professional kidnappers. The tree under which the answer was to be left—and the money later on—was close to the road fence with big, bare fields on all sides. If a gang of constables should be watching for any one to come for the note they could see him a long way off crossing the fields or in the road. But no, sirree! At half-past eight I was up in that tree as well hidden as a tree toad, waiting for the messenger to arrive.

Exactly on time, a half-grown boy rides up the road on a bicycle, locates the pasteboard box at the foot of the fence-post, slips a folded piece of paper into it and pedals away again back toward Summit.

I waited an hour and then concluded the thing was square. I slid down the tree, got the note, slipped along the fence till I struck the woods, and was back at the cave in another half an hour. I opened the note, got near the lantern and read it to Bill. It was written with a pen in a crabbed hand, and the sum and substance of it was this:

Two Desperate Men.

Gentlemen: I received your letter to-day by post, in regard to the ransom you ask for the return of my son. I think you are a little high in your demands, and I hereby make you a counter-proposition, which I am inclined to believe you will accept. You bring Johnny home and pay me two hundred and fifty dollars in cash, and I agree to take him off your hands. You had better come at night, for the neighbours believe he is lost, and I couldn't be responsible for what they would do to anybody they saw bringing him back.

Very respectfully,
EBENEZER DORSET.

"Great pirates of Penzance!" says I; "of all the impudent—"
But I glanced at Bill, and hesitated. He had the most appealing look in his eyes I ever saw on the face of a dumb or a talking brute.
"Sam," says he, "what's two hundred and fifty dollars, after all? We've got the money. One more night of this kid will send me to a bed in Bedlam. Besides being a thorough gentleman, I think Mr. Dorset is a spendthrift for making us such a liberal offer. You ain't going to let the chance go, are you?"
"Tell you the truth, Bill," says I, "this little he ewe lamb has somewhat got on my nerves too. We'll take him home, pay the ransom and make our get-away."
We took him home that night. We got him to go by telling him that his father had bought a silver-mounted rifle and a pair of moccasins for him, and we were going to hunt bears the next day.
It was just twelve o'clock when we knocked at Ebenezer's front door. Just at the moment when I should have been abstracting the fifteen hundred dollars from the box under the tree, according to the original proposition, Bill was counting out two hundred and fifty dollars into Dorset's hand.
When the kid found out we were going to leave him at home he started up a howl like a calliope and fastened himself as tight as a leech to Bill's leg. His father peeled him away gradually, like a porous plaster.
"How long can you hold him?" asks Bill.
"I'm not as strong as I used to be," says old Dorset, "but I think I can promise you ten minutes."
"Enough," says Bill. "In ten minutes I shall cross the Central, Southern and Middle Western States, and be legging it trippingly for the Canadian border."
And, as dark as it was, and as fat as Bill was, and as good a runner as I am, he was a good mile and a half out of Summit before I could catch up with him.

Theme/Concept

C3

Write a moral for this story.

Inference

C2

When did you know the kidnappers' plans may not be realized? What phrases or descriptions led you to that conclusion?

Literary Elements

C1

How does O. Henry use language, foreshadowing, and characterization to make the story engaging? Cite specific examples.

THE RANSOM OF RED CHIEF

Creative Synthesis

D3

Write a story about an unprecedented event mimicking the style of O. Henry.

Summarizing

D2

This story has humorous qualities that could be depicted graphically. Create a four-frame comic to summarize the critical and humorous events of the story.

Paraphrasing

D1

O. Henry uses common language of the day. Select at least four phrases that you are unfamiliar with and explain what they mean in your own words.

THE RANSOM OF RED CHIEF

Using Emotion

E3

Sometimes things do not turn out as we planned. How do you know when it is time to persevere and when to quit and cut your losses?

Expressing Emotion

E2

Has there ever been a time that something you did cost you more than you gained? How did you respond?

Understanding Emotion

E1

Who do you most relate to in the story: the boy, the kidnappers, or the boy's father? Why?

THE RANSOM OF RED CHIEF

The Monkey's Paw
by W. W. Jacobs

I

Without, the night was cold and wet, but in the small parlour of Laburnam Villa the blinds were drawn and the fire burned brightly. Father and son were at chess, the former, who possessed ideas about the game involving radical changes, putting his king into such sharp and unnecessary perils that it even provoked comment from the white-haired old lady knitting placidly by the fire.

"Hark at the wind," said Mr. White, who, having seen a fatal mistake after it was too late, was amiably desirous of preventing his son from seeing it.

"I'm listening," said the latter, grimly surveying the board as he stretched out his hand. "Check."

"I should hardly think that he'd come to-night," said his father, with his hand poised over the board.

"Mate," replied the son.

"That's the worst of living so far out," bawled Mr. White, with sudden and unlooked-for violence; "of all the beastly, slushy, out-of-the-way places to live in, this is the worst. Pathway's a bog, and the road's a torrent. I don't know what people are thinking about. I suppose because only two houses on the road are let, they think it doesn't matter."

"Never mind, dear," said his wife soothingly; "perhaps you'll win the next one."

Mr. White looked up sharply, just in time to intercept a knowing glance between mother and son. The words died away on his lips, and he hid a guilty grin in his thin grey beard.

"There he is," said Herbert White, as the gate banged to loudly and heavy footsteps came toward the door.

The old man rose with hospitable haste, and opening the door, was heard condoling with the new arrival. The new arrival also condoled with himself, so that Mrs. White said, "Tut, tut!" and coughed gently as her husband entered the room, followed by a tall burly man, beady of eye and rubicund of visage.

"Sergeant-Major Morris," he said, introducing him.

The sergeant-major shook hands, and taking the proffered seat by the fire, watched contentedly while his host got out whisky and tumblers and stood a small copper kettle on the fire.

At the third glass his eyes got brighter, and he began to talk, the little family circle regarding with eager interest this visitor from distant parts, as he squared his broad shoulders in the chair and spoke of strange scenes and doughty deeds; of wars and plagues and strange peoples.

"Twenty-one years of it," said Mr. White, nodding at his wife and son. "When he went away he was a slip of a youth in the warehouse. Now look at him."

"He don't look to have taken much harm," said Mrs. White, politely.

"I'd like to go to India myself," said the old man, "just to look round a bit, you know."

"Better where you are," said the sergeant-major, shaking his head. He put down the empty glass, and sighing softly, shook it again.

"I should like to see those old temples and fakirs and jugglers," said the old man. "What was that you started telling me the other day about a monkey's paw or something, Morris?"

"Nothing," said the soldier hastily. "Leastways, nothing worth hearing."

"Monkey's paw?" said Mrs. White curiously.

"Well, it's just a bit of what you might call magic, perhaps," said the sergeant-major off-handedly.

His three listeners leaned forward eagerly. The visitor absentmindedly put his empty glass to his lips and then set it down again. His host filled it for him.

"To look at," said the sergeant-major, fumbling in his pocket, "it's just an ordinary little paw, dried to a mummy."

He took something out of his pocket and proffered it. Mrs. White drew back with a grimace, but her son, taking it, examined it curiously.

"And what is there special about it?" inquired Mr. White, as he took it from his son and, having examined it, placed it upon the table.

"It had a spell put on it by an old fakir," said the sergeant-major, "a very holy man. He wanted to show that fate ruled people's lives, and that those who interfered with it did so to their sorrow. He put a spell on it so that three separate men could each have three wishes from it."

His manner was so impressive that his hearers were conscious that their light laughter jarred somewhat.

"Well, why don't you have three, sir?" said Herbert White cleverly.

The soldier regarded him in the way that middle age is wont to regard presumptuous youth. "I have," he said quietly, and his blotchy face whitened.

"And did you really have the three wishes granted?" asked Mrs. White.

"I did," said the sergeant-major, and his glass tapped against his strong teeth.

"And has anybody else wished?" inquired the old lady.

"The first man had his three wishes, yes," was the reply. "I don't know what the first two were, but the third was for death. That's how I got the paw."

His tones were so grave that a hush fell upon the group.

"If you've had your three wishes, it's no good to you now, then, Morris," said the old man at last. "What do you keep it for?"

The soldier shook his head. "Fancy, I suppose," he said slowly.

"If you could have another three wishes," said the old man, eyeing him keenly, "would you have them?"

"I don't know," said the other. "I don't know."

He took the paw, and dangling it between his front finger and thumb, suddenly threw it upon the fire. White, with a slight cry, stooped down and snatched it off.

"Better let it burn," said the soldier solemnly.

"If you don't want it, Morris," said the old man, "give it to me."

"I won't," said his friend doggedly. "I threw it on the fire. If you keep it, don't blame me for what happens. Pitch it on the fire again, like a sensible man."

The other shook his head and examined his new possession closely. "How do you do it?" he inquired.

"Hold it up in your right hand and wish aloud," said the sergeant-major, "but I warn you of the consequences."

"Sounds like the Arabian Nights," said Mrs. White, as she rose and began to set the supper. "Don't you think you might wish for four pairs of hands for me?"

Her husband drew the talisman from his pocket and then all three burst into laughter as the sergeant-major, with a look of alarm on his face, caught him by the arm.

"If you must wish," he said gruffly, "wish for something sensible."

Mr. White dropped it back into his pocket, and placing chairs, motioned his friend to the table. In the business of supper the talisman was partly forgotten, and afterward the three sat listening in an enthralled fashion to a second instalment of the soldier's adventures in India.

"If the tale about the monkey paw is not more truthful than those he has been telling us," said Herbert, as the door closed behind their guest, just in time for him to catch the last train, "we shan't make much out of it."

"Did you give him anything for it, father?" inquired Mrs. White, regarding her husband closely.

"A trifle," said he, colouring slightly. "He didn't want it, but I made him take it. And he pressed me again to throw it away."

"Likely," said Herbert, with pretended horror. "Why, we're going to be rich, and famous, and happy. Wish to be an emperor, father, to begin with; then you can't be henpecked."

He darted round the table, pursued by the maligned Mrs. White armed with an antimacassar.

Mr. White took the paw from his pocket and eyed it dubiously. "I don't know what to wish for, and that's a fact," he said slowly. "It seems to me I've got all I want."

"If you only cleared the house, you'd be quite happy, wouldn't you?" said Herbert, with his hand on his shoulder. "Well, wish for two hundred pounds, then; that'll just do it."

His father, smiling shamefacedly at his own credulity, held up the talisman, as his son, with a solemn face somewhat marred by a wink at his mother, sat down at the piano and struck a few impressive chords.

"I wish for two hundred pounds," said the old man distinctly.

A fine crash from the piano greeted the words, interrupted by a shuddering cry from the old man. His wife and son ran toward him.

"It moved," he cried, with a glance of disgust at the object as it lay on the floor. "As I wished it twisted in my hands like a snake."

"Well, I don't see the money," said his son, as he picked it up and placed it on the table, "and I bet I never shall."

"It must have been your fancy, father," said his wife, regarding him anxiously.

He shook his head. "Never mind, though; there's no harm done, but it gave me a shock all the same."

They sat down by the fire again while the two men finished their pipes. Outside, the wind was higher than ever, and the old man started nervously at the sound of a door banging upstairs. A silence unusual and depressing settled upon all three, which lasted until the old couple rose to retire for the night.

"I expect you'll find the cash tied up in a big bag in the middle of your bed," said Herbert, as he bade them good-night, "and something horrible squatting up on top of the wardrobe watching you as you pocket your ill-gotten gains."

He sat alone in the darkness, gazing at the dying fire, and seeing faces in it. The last face was so horrible and so simian that he gazed at it in amazement. It got so vivid that, with a little uneasy laugh, he felt on the table for a glass containing a little water to throw over it. His hand grasped the monkey's paw, and with a little shiver he wiped his hand on his coat and went up to bed.

II

In the brightness of the wintry sun next morning as it streamed over the breakfast table Herbert laughed at his fears. There was an air of prosaic wholesomeness about the room which it had lacked on the previous night, and the dirty, shrivelled little paw was pitched on the sideboard with a carelessness which betokened no great belief in its virtues.

"I suppose all old soldiers are the same," said Mrs. White. "The idea of our listening to such nonsense! How could wishes be granted in these days? And if they could, how could two hundred pounds hurt you, father?"

"Might drop on his head from the sky," said the frivolous Herbert.

"Morris said the things happened so naturally," said his father, "that you might if you so wished attribute it to coincidence."

"Well, don't break into the money before I come back," said Herbert, as he rose from the table. "I'm afraid it'll turn you into a mean, avaricious man, and we shall have to disown you."

His mother laughed, and following him to the door, watched him down the road, and returning to the breakfast table, was very happy at the expense of her husband's credulity. All of which did not prevent her from scurrying to the door at the postman's knock, nor prevent her from referring somewhat shortly to retired sergeant-majors of bibulous habits when she found that the post brought a tailor's bill.

"Herbert will have some more of his funny remarks, I expect, when he comes home," she said, as they sat at dinner.

"I dare say," said Mr. White, pouring himself out some beer; "but for all that, the thing moved in my hand; that I'll swear to."

"You thought it did," said the old lady soothingly.

"I say it did," replied the other. "There was no thought about it; I had just—What's the matter?"

His wife made no reply. She was watching the mysterious movements of a man outside, who, peering in an undecided fashion at the house, appeared to be trying to make up his mind to enter. In mental connection with the two hundred pounds, she noticed that the stranger was well dressed and wore a silk hat of glossy newness. Three times he paused at the gate, and then walked on again. The fourth time he stood with his hand upon it, and then with sudden resolution flung it open and walked up the path. Mrs. White at the same moment placed her hands behind her, and hurriedly unfastening the strings of her apron, put that useful article of apparel beneath the cushion of her chair.

She brought the stranger, who seemed ill at ease, into the room. He gazed at her furtively, and listened in a preoccupied fashion as the old lady apologized for the appearance of the room, and her husband's coat, a garment which he usually reserved for the garden. She then waited as patiently as her sex would permit, for him to broach his business, but he was at first strangely silent.

"I—was asked to call," he said at last, and stooped and picked a piece of cotton from his trousers. "I come from Maw and Meggins."

The old lady started. "Is anything the matter?" she asked breathlessly. "Has anything happened to Herbert? What is it? What is it?"

Her husband interposed. "There, there, mother," he said hastily. "Sit down, and don't jump to conclusions. You've not brought bad news, I'm sure, sir" and he eyed the other wistfully.

"I'm sorry—" began the visitor.

"Is he hurt?" demanded the mother.

The visitor bowed in assent. "Badly hurt," he said quietly, "but he is not in any pain."

"Oh, thank God!" said the old woman, clasping her hands. "Thank God for that! Thank—"

She broke off suddenly as the sinister meaning of the assurance dawned upon her and she saw the awful confirmation of her fears in the other's averted face. She caught her breath, and turning to her slower-witted husband, laid her trembling old hand upon his. There was a long silence.

"He was caught in the machinery," said the visitor at length, in a low voice.

"Caught in the machinery," repeated Mr. White, in a dazed fashion, "yes."

He sat staring blankly out at the window, and taking his wife's hand between his own, pressed it as he had been wont to do in their old courting days nearly forty years before.

"He was the only one left to us," he said, turning gently to the visitor. "It is hard."

The other coughed, and rising, walked slowly to the window. "The firm wished me to convey their sincere sympathy with you in your great loss," he said, without looking round. "I beg that you will understand I am only their servant and merely obeying orders."

There was no reply; the old woman's face was white, her eyes staring, and her breath inaudible; on the husband's face was a look such as his friend the sergeant might have carried into his first action.

"I was to say that Maw and Meggins disclaim all responsibility," continued the other. "They admit no liability at all, but in consideration of your son's services they wish to present you with a certain sum as compensation."

Mr. White dropped his wife's hand, and rising to his feet, gazed with a look of horror at his visitor. His dry lips shaped the words, "How much?"

"Two hundred pounds," was the answer.

Unconscious of his wife's shriek, the old man smiled faintly, put out his hands like a sightless man, and dropped, a senseless heap, to the floor.

III

In the huge new cemetery, some two miles distant, the old people buried their dead, and came back to a house steeped in shadow and silence. It was all over so quickly that at first they could hardly realize it, and remained in a state of expectation as though of something else to happen—something else which was to lighten this load, too heavy for old hearts to bear.

But the days passed, and expectation gave place to resignation—the hopeless resignation of the old, sometimes miscalled, apathy. Sometimes they hardly exchanged a word, for now they had nothing to talk about, and their days were long to weariness.

It was about a week after that that the old man, waking suddenly in the night, stretched out his hand and found himself alone. The room was in darkness, and the sound of subdued weeping came from the window. He raised himself in bed and listened.

"Come back," he said tenderly. "You will be cold."

"It is colder for my son," said the old woman, and wept afresh.

The sound of her sobs died away on his ears. The bed was warm, and his eyes heavy with sleep. He dozed fitfully, and then slept until a sudden wild cry from his wife awoke him with a start.

"The paw!" she cried wildly. "The monkey's paw!"

He started up in alarm. "Where? Where is it? What's the matter?"

She came stumbling across the room toward him. "I want it," she said quietly. "You've not destroyed it?"

"It's in the parlour, on the bracket," he replied, marvelling. "Why?"

She cried and laughed together, and bending over, kissed his cheek.

"I only just thought of it," she said hysterically. "Why didn't I think of it before? Why didn't you think of it?"

"Think of what?" he questioned.

"The other two wishes," she replied rapidly. "We've only had one."

"Was not that enough?" he demanded fiercely.

"No," she cried, triumphantly; "we'll have one more. Go down and get it quickly, and wish our boy alive again."

The man sat up in bed and flung the bedclothes from his quaking limbs. "Good God, you are mad!" he cried aghast.

"Get it," she panted; "get it quickly, and wish—Oh, my boy, my boy!"

Her husband struck a match and lit the candle. "Get back to bed," he said, unsteadily. "You don't know what you are saying."

"We had the first wish granted," said the old woman, feverishly; "why not the second."

"A coincidence," stammered the old man.

"Go and get it and wish," cried the old woman, quivering with excitement.

The old man turned and regarded her, and his voice shook. "He has been dead ten days, and besides he—I would not tell you else, but—I could only recognize him by his clothing. If he was too terrible for you to see then, how now?"

"Bring him back," cried the old woman, and dragged him toward the door. "Do you think I fear the child I have nursed?"

He went down in the darkness, and felt his way to the parlour, and then to the mantelpiece. The talisman was in its place, and a horrible fear that the unspoken wish might bring his mutilated son before him ere he could escape from the room seized upon him, and he caught his breath as he found that he had lost the direction of the door. His brow cold with sweat, he felt his way round the table, and groped along the wall until he found himself in the small passage with the unwholesome thing in his hand.

Even his wife's face seemed changed as he entered the room. It was white and expectant, and to his fears seemed to have an unnatural look upon it. He was afraid of her.

"Wish!" she cried, in a strong voice.

"It is foolish and wicked," he faltered.

"Wish!" repeated his wife.

He raised his hand. "I wish my son alive again."

The talisman fell to the floor, and he regarded it fearfully. Then he sank trembling into a chair as the old woman, with burning eyes, walked to the window and raised the blind.

He sat until he was chilled with the cold, glancing occasionally at the figure of the old woman peering through the window. The candle end, which had burnt below the rim of the china candlestick, was throwing pulsating shadows on the ceiling and walls, until, with a flicker larger than the rest, it expired. The old man, with an unspeakable sense of relief at the failure of the talisman, crept back to his bed, and a minute or two afterward the old woman came silently and apathetically beside him.

Neither spoke, but both lay silently listening to the ticking of the clock. A stair creaked, and a squeaky mouse scurried noisily through the wall. The darkness was oppressive, and after lying for some time screwing up his courage, the husband took the box of matches, and striking one, went downstairs for a candle.

At the foot of the stairs the match went out, and he paused to strike another, and at the same moment a knock, so quiet and stealthy as to be scarcely audible, sounded on the front door.

The matches fell from his hand. He stood motionless, his breath suspended until the knock was repeated. Then he turned and fled swiftly back to his room, and closed the door behind him. A third knock sounded through the house.

"What's that?" cried the old woman, starting up.

"A rat," said the old man, in shaking tones—"a rat. It passed me on the stairs."

His wife sat up in bed listening. A loud knock resounded through the house.

"It's Herbert!" she screamed. "It's Herbert!"

She ran to the door, but her husband was before her, and catching her by the arm, held her tightly.

"What are you going to do?" he whispered hoarsely.

"It's my boy; it's Herbert!" she cried, struggling mechanically. "I forgot it was two miles away. What are you holding me for? Let go. I must open the door."

"For God's sake, don't let it in," cried the old man trembling.

"You're afraid of your own son," she cried, struggling. "Let me go. I'm coming, Herbert; I'm coming."

There was another knock, and another. The old woman with a sudden wrench broke free and ran from the room. Her husband followed to the landing, and called after her appealingly as she hurried downstairs. He heard the chain rattle back and the bottom bolt drawn slowly and stiffly from the socket. Then the old woman's voice, strained and panting.

"The bolt," she cried loudly. "Come down. I can't reach it."

But her husband was on his hands and knees groping wildly on the floor in search of the paw. If he could only find it before the thing outside got in. A perfect fusillade of knocks reverberated through the house, and he heard the scraping of a chair as his wife put it down in the passage against the door. He heard the creaking of the bolt as it came slowly back, and at the same moment he found the monkey's paw, and frantically breathed his third and last wish.

The knocking ceased suddenly, although the echoes of it were still in the house. He heard the chair drawn back and the door opened. A cold wind rushed up the staircase, and a long loud wail of disappointment and misery from his wife gave him courage to run down to her side, and then to the gate beyond. The street lamp flickering opposite shone on a quiet and deserted road.

Consequences and Implications

A3

Explain the implications and consequences of choices we make and how those affect others. Link your insights from the story to a personal situation.

Cause and Effect

A2

Why did the sergeant present the monkey paw to the family when he knew it was evil?

Sequencing

A1

What are the five most critical events in the story? Sequence them.

THE MONKEY'S PAW

Generalizations

B3

Write three generalizations about this story that show
the relationship between greed and happiness.

Classifications

B2

Detail the events of the story that show greed and that show
happiness. Create a T-chart to categorize your ideas.

Details

B1

How would you describe the family in this
story, based on the details provided?

THE MONKEY'S PAW

Creative Synthesis

D3

Is this story a fairy tale? Why or why not? Write a persuasive essay to convince someone of your opinion.

Summarizing

D2

Create two columns on a piece of paper. In Column 1, write the elements of a fairy tale from D1. In Column 2, summarize events from the story that match the elements of a fairy tale from the first column. Do you have a match from the story for every element? Why or why not?

Paraphrasing

D1

What are the basic elements of a fairy tale? Describe them in your own words.

THE MONKEY'S PAW

The Diamond Necklace

by Guy de Maupassant

The girl was one of those pretty and charming young creatures who sometimes are born, as if by a slip of fate, into a family of clerks. She had no dowry, no expectations, no way of being known, understood, loved, married by any rich and distinguished man; so she let herself be married to a little clerk of the Ministry of Public Instruction.

She dressed plainly because she could not dress well, but she was unhappy as if she had really fallen from a higher station; since with women there is neither caste nor rank, for beauty, grace and charm take the place of family and birth. Natural ingenuity, instinct for what is elegant, a supple mind are their sole hierarchy, and often make of women of the people the equals of the very greatest ladies.

Mathilde suffered ceaselessly, feeling herself born to enjoy all delicacies and all luxuries. She was distressed at the poverty of her dwelling, at the bareness of the walls, at the shabby chairs, the ugliness of the curtains. All those things, of which another woman of her rank would never even have been conscious, tortured her and made her angry. The sight of the little Breton peasant who did her humble housework aroused in her despairing regrets and bewildering dreams. She thought of silent antechambers hung with Oriental tapestry, illumined by tall bronze candelabra, and of two great footmen in knee breeches who sleep in the big armchairs, made drowsy by the oppressive heat of the stove. She thought of long reception halls hung with ancient silk, of the dainty cabinets containing priceless curiosities and of the little coquettish perfumed reception rooms made for chatting at five o'clock with intimate friends, with men famous and sought after, whom all women envy and whose attention they all desire.

When she sat down to dinner, before the round table covered with a tablecloth in use three days, opposite her husband, who uncovered the soup tureen and declared with a delighted air, "Ah, the good soup! I don't know anything better than that," she thought of dainty dinners, of shining silverware, of tapestry that peopled the walls with ancient personages and with strange birds flying in the midst of a fairy forest; and she thought of delicious dishes served on marvelous plates and of the whispered gallantries to which you listen with a sphinxlike smile while you are eating the pink meat of a trout or the wings of a quail.

She had no gowns, no jewels, nothing. And she loved nothing but that. She felt made for that. She would have liked so much to please, to be envied, to be charming, to be sought after.

She had a friend, a former schoolmate at the convent, who was rich, and whom she did not like to go to see any more because she felt so sad when she came home.

But one evening her husband reached home with a triumphant air and holding a large envelope in his hand.

"There," said he, "there is something for you."

She tore the paper quickly and drew out a printed card which bore these words:

> The Minister of Public Instruction and Madame Georges Ramponneau request the honor of M. and Madame Loisel's company at the palace of the Ministry on Monday evening, January 18th.

Instead of being delighted, as her husband had hoped, she threw the invitation on the table crossly, muttering:

"What do you wish me to do with that?"

"Why, my dear, I thought you would be glad. You never go out, and this is such a fine opportunity. I had great trouble to get it. Every one wants to go; it is very select, and they are not giving many invitations to clerks. The whole official world will be there."

She looked at him with an irritated glance and said impatiently:

"And what do you wish me to put on my back?"

He had not thought of that. He stammered:

"Why, the gown you go to the theatre in. It looks very well to me."

He stopped, distracted, seeing that his wife was weeping. Two great tears ran slowly from the corners of her eyes toward the corners of her mouth.

"What's the matter? What's the matter?" he answered.

By a violent effort she conquered her grief and replied in a calm voice, while she wiped her wet cheeks:

"Nothing. Only I have no gown, and, therefore, I can't go to this ball. Give your card to some colleague whose wife is better equipped than I am."

He was in despair. He resumed:

"Come, let us see, Mathilde. How much would it cost, a suitable gown, which you could use on other occasions—something very simple?"

She reflected several seconds, making her calculations and wondering also what sum she could ask without drawing on herself an immediate refusal and a frightened exclamation from the economical clerk.

Finally she replied hesitating:

"I don't know exactly, but I think I could manage it with four hundred francs."

He grew a little pale, because he was laying aside just that amount to buy a gun and treat himself to a little shooting next summer on the plain of Nanterre, with several friends who went to shoot larks there of a Sunday.

But he said:

"Very well. I will give you four hundred francs. And try to have a pretty gown."

The day of the ball drew near and Madame Loisel seemed sad, uneasy, anxious. Her frock was ready, however. Her husband said to her one evening:

"What is the matter? Come, you have seemed very queer these last three days."

And she answered:

"It annoys me not to have a single piece of jewelry, not a single ornament, nothing to put on. I shall look poverty-stricken. I would almost rather not go at all."

"You might wear natural flowers," said her husband. "They're very stylish at this time of year. For ten francs you can get two or three magnificent roses."

She was not convinced.

"No; there's nothing more humiliating than to look poor among other women who are rich."

"How stupid you are!" her husband cried. "Go look up your friend, Madame Forestier, and ask her to lend you some jewels. You're intimate enough with her to do that."

She uttered a cry of joy:

"True! I never thought of it."

The next day she went to her friend and told her of her distress.

Madame Forestier went to a wardrobe with a mirror, took out a large jewel box, brought it back, opened it and said to Madame Loisel:

"Choose, my dear."

She saw first some bracelets, then a pearl necklace, then a Venetian gold cross set with precious stones, of admirable workmanship. She tried on the ornaments before the mirror, hesitated and could not make up her mind to part with them, to give them back. She kept asking:

"Haven't you any more?"

"Why, yes. Look further; I don't know what you like."

Suddenly she discovered, in a black satin box, a superb diamond necklace, and her heart throbbed with an immoderate desire. Her hands trembled as she took it. She fastened it round her throat, outside her high-necked waist, and was lost in ecstasy at her reflection in the mirror.

Then she asked, hesitating, filled with anxious doubt:

"Will you lend me this, only this?"

"Why, yes, certainly."

She threw her arms round her friend's neck, kissed her passionately, then fled with her treasure.

The night of the ball arrived. Madame Loisel was a great success. She was prettier than any other woman present, elegant, graceful, smiling and wild with joy. All the men looked at her, asked her name, sought to be introduced. All the attaches of the Cabinet wished to waltz with her. She was remarked by the minister himself.

She danced with rapture, with passion, intoxicated by pleasure, forgetting all in the triumph of her beauty, in the glory of her success, in a sort of cloud of happiness comprised of all this homage, admiration, these awakened desires and of that sense of triumph which is so sweet to woman's heart.

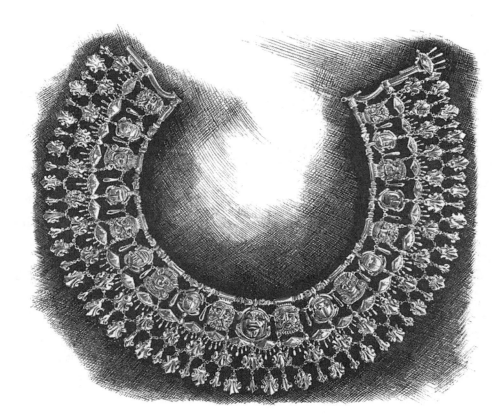

She left the ball about four o'clock in the morning. Her husband had been sleeping since midnight in a little deserted anteroom with three other gentlemen whose wives were enjoying the ball.

He threw over her shoulders the wraps he had brought, the modest wraps of common life, the poverty of which contrasted with the elegance of the ball dress. She felt this and wished to escape so as not to be remarked by the other women, who were enveloping themselves in costly furs.

Loisel held her back, saying: "Wait a bit. You will catch cold outside. I will call a cab."

But she did not listen to him and rapidly descended the stairs. When they reached the street they could not find a carriage and began to look for one, shouting after the cabmen passing at a distance.

They went toward the Seine in despair, shivering with cold. At last they found on the quay one of those ancient night cabs which, as though they were ashamed to show their shabbiness during the day, are never seen round Paris until after dark.

It took them to their dwelling in the Rue des Martyrs, and sadly they mounted the stairs to their flat. All was ended for her. As to him, he reflected that he must be at the ministry at ten o'clock that morning.

She removed her wraps before the glass so as to see herself once more in all her glory. But suddenly she uttered a cry. She no longer had the necklace around her neck!

"What is the matter with you?" demanded her husband, already half undressed.

She turned distractedly toward him.

"I have—I have—I've lost Madame Forestier's necklace," she cried.

He stood up, bewildered.

"What!—how? Impossible!"

They looked among the folds of her skirt, of her cloak, in her pockets, everywhere, but did not find it.

"You're sure you had it on when you left the ball?" he asked.

"Yes, I felt it in the vestibule of the minister's house."

"But if you had lost it in the street we should have heard it fall. It must be in the cab."

"Yes, probably. Did you take his number?"

"No. And you—didn't you notice it?"

"No."

They looked, thunderstruck, at each other. At last Loisel put on his clothes.

"I shall go back on foot," said he, "over the whole route, to see whether I can find it."

He went out. She sat waiting on a chair in her ball dress, without strength to go to bed, overwhelmed, without any fire, without a thought.

Her husband returned about seven o'clock. He had found nothing.

He went to police headquarters, to the newspaper offices to offer a reward; he went to the cab companies—everywhere, in fact, whither he was urged by the least spark of hope.

She waited all day, in the same condition of mad fear before this terrible calamity.

Loisel returned at night with a hollow, pale face. He had discovered nothing.

"You must write to your friend," said he, "that you have broken the clasp of her necklace and that you are having it mended. That will give us time to turn round."

She wrote at his dictation.

At the end of a week they had lost all hope. Loisel, who had aged five years, declared:

"We must consider how to replace that ornament."

The next day they took the box that had contained it and went to the jeweler whose name was found within. He consulted his books.

"It was not I, madame, who sold that necklace; I must simply have furnished the case."

Then they went from jeweler to jeweler, searching for a necklace like the other, trying to recall it, both sick with chagrin and grief.

They found, in a shop at the Palais Royal, a string of diamonds that seemed to them exactly like the one they had lost. It was worth forty thousand francs. They could have it for thirty-six.

So they begged the jeweler not to sell it for three days yet. And they made a bargain that he should buy it back for thirty-four thousand francs, in case they should find the lost necklace before the end of February.

Loisel possessed eighteen thousand francs which his father had left him. He would borrow the rest.

He did borrow, asking a thousand francs of one, five hundred of another, five louis here, three louis there. He gave notes, took up ruinous obligations, dealt with usurers and all the race of lenders. He compromised all the rest of his life, risked signing a note without even knowing whether he could meet it; and, frightened by the trouble yet to come, by the black misery that was about to fall upon him, by the prospect of all the physical privations and moral tortures that he was to suffer, he went to get the new necklace, laying upon the jeweler's counter thirty-six thousand francs.

When Madame Loisel took back the necklace Madame Forestier said to her with a chilly manner:

"You should have returned it sooner; I might have needed it."

She did not open the case, as her friend had so much feared. If she had detected the substitution, what would she have thought, what would she have said? Would she not have taken Madame Loisel for a thief?

Thereafter Madame Loisel knew the horrible existence of the needy. She bore her part, however, with sudden heroism. That dreadful debt must be paid. She would pay it. They dismissed their servant; they changed their lodgings; they rented a garret under the roof.

She came to know what heavy housework meant and the odious cares of the kitchen. She washed the dishes, using her dainty fingers and rosy nails on greasy pots and pans. She washed the soiled linen, the shirts and the dishcloths, which she dried upon a line; she carried the slops down to the street every morning and carried up the water, stopping for breath at every landing. And dressed like a woman of the people, she went to the fruiterer, the grocer, the butcher, a basket on her arm, bargaining, meeting with impertinence, defending her miserable money, sou by sou.

Every month they had to meet some notes, renew others, obtain more time.

Her husband worked evenings, making up a tradesman's accounts, and late at night he often copied manuscript for five sous a page.

This life lasted ten years.

At the end of ten years they had paid everything, everything, with the rates of usury and the accumulations of the compound interest.

Madame Loisel looked old now. She had become the woman of impoverished households—strong and hard and rough. With frowsy hair, skirts askew and red hands, she talked loud while washing the floor with great swishes of water. But sometimes, when her husband was at the office, she sat down near the window and she thought of that gay evening of long ago, of that ball where she had been so beautiful and so admired.

What would have happened if she had not lost that necklace? Who knows? Who knows? How strange and changeful is life! How small a thing is needed to make or ruin us!

But one Sunday, having gone to take a walk in the Champs Elysees to refresh herself after the labors of the week, she suddenly perceived a woman who was leading a child. It was Madame Forestier, still young, still beautiful, still charming.

Madame Loisel felt moved. Should she speak to her? Yes, certainly. And now that she had paid, she would tell her all about it. Why not?

She went up.

"Good-day, Jeanne."

The other, astonished to be familiarly addressed by this plain good-wife, did not recognize her at all and stammered:

"But—madame!—I do not know—You must have mistaken."

"No. I am Mathilde Loisel."

Her friend uttered a cry.

"Oh, my poor Mathilde! How you are changed!"

"Yes, I have had a pretty hard life, since I last saw you, and great poverty—and that because of you!"

"Of me! How so?"

"Do you remember that diamond necklace you lent me to wear at the ministerial ball?"

"Yes. Well?"

"Well, I lost it."

"What do you mean? You brought it back."

"I brought you back another exactly like it. And it has taken us ten years to pay for it. You can understand that it was not easy for us, for us who had nothing. At last it is ended, and I am very glad."

Madame Forestier had stopped.

"You say that you bought a necklace of diamonds to replace mine?"

"Yes. You never noticed it, then! They were very similar."

And she smiled with a joy that was at once proud and ingenuous.

Madame Forestier, deeply moved, took her hands.

"Oh, my poor Mathilde! Why, my necklace was paste! It was worth at most only five hundred francs!"

Consequences and Implications

A3

What are the consequences of never being happy with what you have, according to de Maupassant?

Cause and Effect

A2

What are the cause and effect relationships in this story? Which one is most significant? Why?

Sequencing

A1

Make an outline of the most important events of the story. Explain why the events you listed are the most important.

THE DIAMOND NECKLACE

Theme/Concept

C3

What message do you think de Maupassant wanted to convey? Why? How are the themes of love and beauty used in the story by de Maupassant?

Inference

C2

What does this story suggest about friendship? About satisfaction? About beauty? What can we infer about the meaning of the story from its ending?

Literary Elements

C1

How is the characterization of Mathilde important to the meaning of this story? What qualities does she possess?

THE DIAMOND NECKLACE

Using Emotion

E3

How did emotion drive the telling of the story? Explain your answer using evidence from the text.

Expressing Emotion

E2

When should you be satisfied with what you have and when should you strive for something better? How are your thoughts similar to or different from the characters in the story?

Understanding Emotion

E1

How did you feel at the end of the story? Why?

THE DIAMOND NECKLACE

The Celebrated Jumping Frog of Calaveras County

by Mark Twain

Mr. A. Ward,

Dear Sir:—Well, I called on good-natured, garrulous old Simon Wheeler, and inquired after your friend, Leonidas W. Smiley, as you requested me to do, and I hereunto append the result. If you can get any information out of it you are cordially welcome to it. I have a lurking suspicion that your Leonidas W. Smiley is a myth—that you never knew such a personage, and that you only conjectured that if I asked old Wheeler about him it would remind him of his infamous *Jim* Smiley, and he would go to work and bore me nearly to death with some infernal reminiscence of him as long and tedious as it should be useless to me. If that was your design, Mr. Ward, it will gratify you to know that it succeeded.

I found Simon Wheeler dozing comfortably by the bar-room stove of the old, dilapidated tavern in the ancient mining camp of Boomerang, and I noticed that he was fat and bald-headed, and had an expression of winning gentleness and simplicity upon his tranquil countenance. He roused up and gave me good-day. I told him a friend of mine had commissioned me to make some inquiries about a cherished companion of his boyhood named Leonidas W. Smiley—Rev. Leonidas W. Smiley—a young minister of the Gospel, who he had heard was at one time a resident of this village of Boomerang. I added that if Mr. Wheeler could tell me any thing about this Rev. Leonidas W. Smiley, I would feel under many obligations to him.

Simon Wheeler backed me into a corner and blockaded me there with his chair—and then sat me down and reeled off the monotonous narrative which follows this paragraph. He never smiled, he never frowned, he never changed his voice from the gentle-flowing key to which he tuned the initial sentence, he never betrayed the slightest suspicion of enthusiasm—but all through the interminable narrative there ran a vein of impressive earnestness and sincerity, which showed me plainly that, so far from his imagining that there was any thing ridiculous or funny about his story, he regarded it as a really important matter, and admired its two heroes as men of transcendent genius in finesse. To me, the spectacle of a man drifting serenely along through such a queer yarn without ever smiling was exquisitely absurd. As I said before, I asked him to tell me what he knew of Rev. Leonidas W. Smiley, and he replied as follows. I let him go on in his own way, and never interrupted him once:

There was a feller here once by the name of *Jim* Smiley, in the winter of '49—or maybe it was the spring of '50—I don't recollect exactly, somehow,

Name: _____ Date: _____

though what makes me think it was one or the other is because I remember the big flume wasn't finished when he first came to the camp; but any way, he was the curiosest man about always betting on any thing that turned up you ever see, if he could get any body to bet on the other side, and if he couldn't he'd change sides—any way that suited the other man would suit *him*—any way just so's he got a bet, *he* was satisfied. But still, he was lucky—uncommon lucky; he most always come out winner. He was always ready and laying for a chance; there couldn't be no solitry thing mentioned but that feller'd offer to bet on it—and take any side you please, as I was just telling you. If there was a horse-race, you'd find him flush, or you'd find him busted at the end of it; if there was a dog-fight, he'd bet on it; if there was a cat-fight, he'd bet on it; if there was a chicken-fight, he'd bet on it; why, if there was two birds setting on a fence, he would bet you which one would fly first—or if there was a camp-meeting, he would be there reglar, to bet on Parson Walker, which he judged to be the best exhorter about here, and so he was, too, and a good man. If he even seen a straddle-bug start to go any wheres, he would bet you how long it would take him to get wher-ever he was going to, and if you took him up, he would foller that straddle-bug to Mexico but what he would find out where he was bound for and how long he was on the road. Lots of the boys here has seen that Smiley, and can tell you about him. Why, it never made no difference to *him*—he would bet on *anything*—the dangdest feller. Parson Walker's wife laid very sick, once, for a good while, and it seemed as if they warn't going to save her; but one morning he come in, and Smiley asked him how she was, and he said she was considerable better—thank the Lord for his inf'nit mercy—and coming on so smart that, with the blessing of Providence, she'd get well yet—and Smiley, before he thought, says, "Well, I'll resk two-and-a-half that she don't, anyway."

Thish-yer Smiley had a mare—the boys called her the fifteen-minute nag, but that was only in fun, you know, because, of course, she was faster than that—and he used to win money on that horse, for all she was so slow and always had the asthma, or the distemper, or the consumption, or something of that kind. They used to give her two or three hundred yards' start, and then pass her under way; but always at the fag-end of the race she'd get excited and desperate-like, and come cavorting and straddling up, and scat-tering her legs around limber, sometimes in the air, and sometimes out to one side amongst the fences, and kicking up m-o-r-e dust, and raising m-o-r-e racket with her coughing and sneezing and blowing her nose—and always fetch up at the stand just about a neck ahead, as near as you could cipher it down.

And he had a little small bull pup, that to look at him you'd think he warn't worth a cent, but to set around and look ornery, and lay for a chance to steal something. But as soon as money was up on him, he was a different dog—his underjaw'd begin to stick out like the fo'castle of a steamboat, and his teeth would uncover, and shine savage like the furnaces. And a dog might tackle him, and bully-rag him, and bite him, and throw him over his shoulder two or three times, and Andrew Jackson—which was the name of the pup—Andrew Jackson would never let on but what he was satisfied, and hadn't expected nothing else—and the bets being doubled and doubled on the other side all the time, till the money was all up—and then all of a sudden he would grab that other dog jest by the j'int of his hind leg and freeze to it—not chaw, you understand, but only jest grip and hang on till they thronged up the sponge, if it was a year. Smiley always come out winner on that pup, till he harnessed a dog once that didn't have no hind legs, because they'd been sawed off in a circular saw, and when the thing had gone along far enough, and the money was all up, and he come to make a snatch for his pet holt, he saw in a minute how he'd been imposed on, and how the other dog had him in the door, so to speak, and he 'peared surprised, and then he looked sorter discouraged-like, and didn't try no more to win the fight, and so he got shucked out bad. He give Smiley a look, as much as to say his heart was broke, and it was *his* fault, for putting up a dog that hadn't no hind legs for him to take holt of, which was his main dependence in a fight, and then he limped off a piece and laid down and died. It was a good pup, was that Andrew Jackson, and would have made a name for hisself if he'd lived, for the stuff was in him, and he had genius—I know it, because he hadn't had no opportunities to speak of, and it don't stand to reason that a dog could make such a fight as he could under them circumstances, if he hadn't no talent. It always makes me feel sorry when I think of that last fight of his'n, and the way it turned out.

Well, thish-yer Smiley had rat-tarriers, and chicken cocks, and tom-cats, and all of them kind of things, till you couldn't rest, and you couldn't fetch nothing for him to bet on but he'd match you. He ketched a frog one day, and took him home, and said he cal'klated to edercate him; and so he never done nothing for three months but set in his back yard and learn that frog to jump. And you bet you he *did* learn him, too. He'd give him a little hunch behind, and the next minute you'd see that frog whirling in the air like a doughnut—see him turn one summerset, or may be a couple, if he got a good start, and come down flat-footed and all right, like a cat. He got him up so in the matter of ketching flies, and kept him in practice so constant, that he'd nail a fly every time as far as he could see him. Smiley said all a frog wanted was education, and he could do most anything—and I believe him. Why, I've seen him set Dan'l Webster down here on this floor—Dan'l Webster was the name of the frog—and sing out, "Flies, Dan'l, flies!" and quicker'n you could wink, he'd spring straight up, and snake a fly off'n the counter there, and flop down on the floor again as solid as a gob of mud, and fall to scratching the side of his head with his hind foot as indifferent as if he hadn't no idea he'd been doin' any more'n any frog might do. You never see a frog so modest and straightfor'ard as he was, for all he was so gifted. And when it come to fair-and-square jumping on a dead level, he could get over more ground at one straddle than any animal of his breed you ever see. Jumping on a dead level was his strong suit, you understand, and when it come to that, Smiley would ante up money on him as long as he had a red. Smiley was monstrous proud of his frog, and well he might be, for fellers that had traveled and ben everywheres, all said he laid over any frog that ever *they* see.

Well, Smiley kept the beast in a little lattice box, and he used to fetch him down town sometimes and lay for a bet. One day a feller—a stranger in the camp, he was—come across him with his box, and says:

"What might it be that you've got in the box?"

And Smiley says, sorter indifferent like, "It might be a parrot, or it might be a canary, may be, but it ain't—it's only just a frog."

And the feller took it, and looked at it careful, and turned it round this way and that, and says, "H'm—so 'tis. Well, what's *he* good for?"

"Well," Smiley says, easy and careless, "He's good enough for *one* thing, I should judge—he can out-jump ary frog in Calaveras county."

The feller took the box again, and took another long, particular look, and give it back to Smiley, and says, very deliberate, "Well—I don't see no p'ints about that frog that's any better'n any other frog."

"Maybe you don't," Smiley says. "Maybe you understand frogs, and maybe you don't understand 'em; maybe you've had experience, and maybe you ain't only a amature, as it were. Anyways, I've got *my* opinion, and I'll resk forty dollars that he can outjump any frog in Calaveras county."

And the feller studied a minute, and then says, kinder sad, like, "Well, I'm only a stranger here, and I ain't got no frog—but if I had a frog, I'd bet you."

And then Smiley says, "That's all right—that's all right—if you'll hold my box a minute, I'll go and get you a frog." And so the feller took the box, and put up his forty dollars along with Smiley's, and set down to wait.

So he set there a good while thinking and thinking to hisself, and then he got the frog out and prized his mouth open and took a tea-spoon and filled him full of quail shot—filled him pretty near up to his chin—and set him on the floor. Smiley he went to the swamp and slopped around in the mud for a long time, and finally he ketched a frog, and fetched him in, and give him to this feller, and says:

"Now if you're ready, set him alongside of Dan'l, with his fore-paws just even with Dan'l's, and I'll give the word." Then he says, "One—two—three—jump!" and him and the feller touched up the frogs from behind, and the new frog hopped off, but Dan'l give a heave, and hysted up his shoulders—so—like a Frenchman, but it wasn't no use—he couldn't budge; he was planted as solid as an anvil, and he couldn't no more stir than if he was anchored out. Smiley was a good deal surprised, and he was disgusted too, but he didn't have no idea what the matter was, of course.

The feller took the money and started away; and when he was going out at the door, he sorter jerked his thumb over his shoulders—this way—at Dan'l, and says again, very deliberate, "Well, *I* don't see no p'ints about that frog that's any better'n any other frog."

Smiley he stood scratching his head and looking down at Dan'l a long time, and at last he says, "I do wonder what in the nation that frog throw'd off for—I wonder if there ain't something the matter with him—he 'pears to look mighty baggy, somehow"—and he ketched Dan'l by the nap of the neck, and lifted him up and says, "Why, blame my cats, if he don't weigh five pound!"—and turned him upside down, and he belched out a double-handful of shot. And then he see how it was, and he was the maddest man—he set the frog down and took out after that feller, but he never ketched him. And—

Here Simon Wheeler heard his name called from the front yard, and got up to go and see what was wanted. And turning to me as he moved away, he said: "Just set where you are, stranger, and rest easy—I an't going to be gone a second."

But, by your leave, I did not think that a continuation of the history of the enterprising vagabond Jim Smiley would be likely to afford me much information concerning the Rev. Leonidas W. Smiley, and so I started away.

At the door I met the sociable Wheeler returning, and he button-holed me and recommenced:

"Well, thish-yer Smiley had a yeller one-eyed cow that didn't have no tail, only jest a short stump like a bannanner, and"

"O, curse Smiley and his afflicted cow!" I muttered, good-naturedly, and bidding the old gentleman good-day, I departed.

Consequences and Implications

A3

What are the implications of the names of the characters in the story? How do those names add to the story's impact?

Cause and Effect

A2

Examine the effects of Twain's use of language on the story. Make a chart with the following three categories: Story Quote, Purpose, and Effect on Reader. Complete the chart using evidence from the text. An example has been started for you.

Story Quote	Purpose	Effect on the Reader
"If there was a . . . he'd bet on it." (Repeated several times.)	Provides foreshadowing about what may happen next	Repetition emphasizes importance

Sequencing

A1

Sequence the events that led up to the contest.

THE CELEBRATED JUMPING FROG OF CALAVERAS COUNTY

THE CELEBRATED JUMPING FROG OF CALAVERAS COUNTY

Theme/Concept

C3

You may have heard the saying "Truth is stranger than fiction." How does Twain keep his reader engaged in the story to make it believable?

Inference

C2

How does Twain use hyperbole and humor to create an entertaining story?

Literary Elements

C1

Find examples of hyperbole and humor in this story. Highlight them in the text.

Creative Synthesis

D3

Many writers are successful because they are able to use events in their own life and adapt them to fictional situations. Write a humorous tale by exaggerating an event from your life.

Summarizing

D2

Summarize the purpose of this story.

Paraphrasing

D1

Paraphrase the ending of this story and its significance.

THE CELEBRATED JUMPING FROG OF CALAVERAS COUNTY

The Lottery Ticket
by Anton Chekhov

⑨④⑨⑨ Lottery Results

Ivan Dmitritch, a middle-class man who lived with his family on an income of twelve hundred a year and was very well satisfied with his lot, sat down on the sofa after supper and began reading the newspaper.

"I forgot to look at the newspaper today," his wife said to him as she cleared the table. "Look and see whether the list of drawings is there."

"Yes, it is," said Ivan Dmitritch; "but hasn't your ticket lapsed?"

"No; I took the interest on Tuesday."

"What is the number?"

"Series 9,499, number 26."

"All right . . . we will look . . . 9,499 and 26."

Ivan Dmitritch had no faith in lottery luck, and would not, as a rule, have consented to look at the lists of winning numbers, but now, as he had nothing else to do and as the newspaper was before his eyes, he passed his finger downwards along the column of numbers. And immediately, as though in mockery of his scepticism, no further than the second line from the top, his eye was caught by the figure 9,499! Unable to believe his eyes, he hurriedly dropped the paper on his knees without looking to see the number of the ticket, and, just as though some one had given him a douche of cold water, he felt an agreeable chill in the pit of the stomach; tingling and terrible and sweet!

"Masha, 9,499 is there!" he said in a hollow voice.

His wife looked at his astonished and panic-stricken face, and realized that he was not joking.

"9,499?" she asked, turning pale and dropping the folded tablecloth on the table.

"Yes, yes . . . it really is there!"

"And the number of the ticket?"

"Oh, yes! There's the number of the ticket too. But stay . . . wait! No, I say! Anyway, the number of our series is there! Anyway, you understand. . . ."

Looking at his wife, Ivan Dmitritch gave a broad, senseless smile, like a baby when a bright object is shown it. His wife smiled too; it was as pleasant to her as to him that he only mentioned the series, and did not try to find out the number of the winning ticket. To torment and tantalize oneself with hopes of possible fortune is so sweet, so thrilling!

"It is our series," said Ivan Dmitritch, after a long silence. "So there is a probability that we have won. It's only a probability, but there it is!"

"Well, now look!"

"Wait a little. We have plenty of time to be disappointed. It's on the second line from the top, so the prize is seventy-five thousand. That's not money, but power, capital! And in a minute I shall look at the list, and there—26! Eh? I say, what if we really have won?"

The husband and wife began laughing and staring at one another in silence. The possibility of winning bewildered them; they could not have said, could not have dreamed, what they both needed that seventy-five thousand for, what they would buy, where they would go. They thought only of the figures 9,499 and 75,000 and pictured them in their imagination, while somehow they could not think of the happiness itself which was so possible.

Ivan Dmitritch, holding the paper in his hand, walked several times from corner to corner, and only when he had recovered from the first impression began dreaming a little.

"And if we have won," he said—"why, it will be a new life, it will be a transformation! The ticket is yours, but if it were mine I should, first of all, of course, spend twenty-five thousand on real property in the shape of an estate; ten thousand on immediate expenses, new furnishing . . . travelling . . . paying debts, and so on. . . . The other forty thousand I would put in the bank and get interest on it."

"Yes, an estate, that would be nice," said his wife, sitting down and dropping her hands in her lap.

"Somewhere in the Tula or Oryol provinces. . . . In the first place we shouldn't need a summer villa, and besides, it would always bring in an income."

And pictures came crowding on his imagination, each more gracious and poetical than the last. And in all these pictures he saw himself well-fed, serene, healthy, felt warm, even hot! Here, after eating a summer soup, cold as ice, he lay on his back on the burning sand close to a stream or in the garden under a lime-tree. . . . It is hot. . . . His little boy and girl are crawling about near him, digging in the sand or catching ladybirds in the grass. He dozes sweetly, thinking of nothing, and feeling all over that he need not go to the office today, tomorrow, or the day after. Or, tired of lying still, he goes to the hayfield, or to the forest for mushrooms, or watches the peasants catching fish with a net. When the sun sets he takes a towel and soap and saunters to the bathing-shed, where he undresses at his leisure, slowly rubs his bare chest with his hands, and goes into the water. And in the water, near the opaque soapy circles, little fish flit to and fro and green water-weeds nod their heads. After bathing there is tea with cream and milk rolls. . . . In the evening a walk or *vint* with the neighbours.

"Yes, it would be nice to buy an estate," said his wife, also dreaming, and from her face it was evident that she was enchanted by her thoughts.

Ivan Dmitritch pictured to himself autumn with its rains, its cold evenings, and its St. Martin's summer. At that season he would have to take longer walks about the garden and beside the river, so as to get thoroughly chilled, and then drink a big glass of vodka and eat a salted mushroom or a soused cucumber, and then—drink another. . . . The children would come running from the kitchen-garden, bringing a carrot and a radish smelling of fresh earth. . . . And then, he would lie stretched full length on the sofa, and in leisurely fashion turn over the pages of some illustrated magazine, or, covering his face with it and unbuttoning his waistcoat, give himself up to slumber.

The St. Martin's summer is followed by cloudy, gloomy weather. It rains day and night, the bare trees weep, the wind is damp and cold. The dogs, the horses, the fowls—all are wet, depressed, downcast. There is nowhere to walk; one can't go out for days together; one has to pace up and down the room, looking despondently at the grey window. It is dreary!

Ivan Dmitritch stopped and looked at his wife.

"I should go abroad, you know, Masha," he said.

And he began thinking how nice it would be in late autumn to go abroad somewhere to the South of France . . . to Italy . . . to India!

"I should certainly go abroad too," his wife said. "But look at the number of the ticket!"

"Wait, wait! . . ."

He walked about the room and went on thinking. It occurred to him: what if his wife really did go abroad? It is pleasant to travel alone, or in the society of light, careless women who live in the present, and not such as think and talk all the journey about nothing but their children, sigh, and tremble with dismay over every farthing. Ivan Dmitritch imagined his wife in the train with a multitude of parcels, baskets, and bags; she would be sighing over something, complaining that the train made her head ache, that she had spent so much money. . . . At the stations he would continually be having to run for boiling water, bread and butter. . . . She wouldn't have dinner because of its being too dear. . . .

"She would begrudge me every farthing," he thought, with a glance at his wife. "The lottery ticket is hers, not mine! Besides, what is the use of her going abroad? What does she want there? She would shut herself up in the hotel, and not let me out of her sight. . . . I know!"

And for the first time in his life his mind dwelt on the fact that his wife had grown elderly and plain, and that she was saturated through and through with the smell of cooking, while he was still young, fresh, and healthy, and might well have got married again.

"Of course, all that is silly nonsense," he thought; "but . . . why should she go abroad? What would she make of it? And yet she would go, of course. . . . I can fancy . . . In reality it is all one to her, whether it is Naples or Klin. She would only be in my way. I should be dependent upon her. I can fancy how, like a regular woman, she will lock the money up as soon as she gets it. . . . She will hide it from me. . . . She will look after her relations and grudge me every farthing."

Ivan Dmitritch thought of her relations. All those wretched brothers and sisters and aunts and uncles would come crawling about as soon as they heard of the winning ticket, would begin whining like beggars, and fawning upon them with oily, hypocritical smiles. Wretched, detestable people! If they were given anything, they would ask for more; while if they were refused, they would swear at them, slander them, and wish them every kind of misfortune.

Ivan Dmitritch remembered his own relations, and their faces, at which he had looked impartially in the past, struck him now as repulsive and hateful.

"They are such reptiles!" he thought.

And his wife's face, too, struck him as repulsive and hateful. Anger surged up in his heart against her, and he thought malignantly:

"She knows nothing about money, and so she is stingy. If she won it she would give me a hundred roubles, and put the rest away under lock and key."

And he looked at his wife, not with a smile now, but with hatred. She glanced at him too, and also with hatred and anger. She had her own day-dreams, her own plans, her own reflections; she understood perfectly well what her husband's dreams were. She knew who would be the first to try and grab her winnings.

"It's very nice making daydreams at other people's expense!" is what her eyes expressed. "No, don't you dare!"

Her husband understood her look; hatred began stirring again in his breast, and in order to annoy his wife he glanced quickly, to spite her at the fourth page on the newspaper and read out triumphantly:

"Series 9,499, number 46! Not 26!"

Hatred and hope both disappeared at once, and it began immediately to seem to Ivan Dmitritch and his wife that their rooms were dark and small and low-pitched, that the supper they had been eating was not doing them good, but lying heavy on their stomachs, that the evenings were long and wearisome. . . .

"What the devil's the meaning of it?" said Ivan Dmitritch, beginning to be ill-humoured. "Wherever one steps there are bits of paper under one's feet, crumbs, husks. The rooms are never swept! One is simply forced to go out. Damnation take my soul entirely! I shall go and hang myself on the first aspen-tree!"

Generalizations

B3

Write three generalizations about happiness based on your categories and examples. How do these generalizations hold true in the story?

Classifications

B2

How would you categorize the relationship between happiness and discontentment? Why?

Details

B1

Cite examples of happiness versus discontentment in the story.

THE LOTTERY TICKET

Theme/Concept

C3

What is the moral of this story?

Inference

C2

Are the characters' beliefs about wealth realistic? Why or why not?

Literary Elements

C1

Explain how the author uses imagery and alliteration to emphasize certain events in the story. When are each used? Why?

THE LOTTERY TICKET

Using Emotion

E3

What is the importance of the lottery ticket on the couple's expectations? Do you have expectations about events that haven't come to fruition? If yes, describe.

Expressing Emotion

E2

Explain a time when an unexpected event changed your life. Was that event positive or negative? How did you react? Predictably? Unpredictably? What lesson did you learn?

Understanding Emotion

E1

Do you think the characters in the story expected their reaction to winning? Why or why not? Use examples from the text.

THE LOTTERY TICKET

CHAPTER 2

Poetry

The following section of *Jacob's Ladder* focuses on selections of classical poetry, both British and American, with corresponding ladders that fit the selection chosen.

The poetry selections with their corresponding ladders are as follows:

Weathers

by Thomas Hardy

This is the weather the cuckoo likes,
And so do I;
When showers betumble the chestnut spikes,
And nestlings fly:
And the little brown nightingale bills his best,
And they sit outside at "The Travellers' Rest,"
And maids come forth sprig-muslin drest,
And citizens dream of the south and west,
And so do I.

II

This is the weather the shepherd shuns,
And so do I;
When beeches drip in brown and duns,
And thresh and ply;
And hill-hid tides throb, throe on throe,
And meadow rivulets overflow,
And drops on gate-bars hang in a row,
And rooks in families homeward go,
And so do I.

Consequences and Implications

A3

Why did Hardy use the phrase "And so do I" so
many times throughout the poem?

Cause and Effect

A2

How does Hardy use cause and effect relationships to create images?

Sequencing

A1

How does the sequence of the last two lines of the first
stanza contribute to the meaning of the poem?

WEATHERS

Creative Synthesis

D3

Create your own poem that consists of two contrasting events. Include a transition statement to link them together.

Summarizing

D2

Compare and contrast the two stanzas of the poem. Explain how they fit together.

Paraphrasing

D1

Draw a picture of Stanza 1 and Stanza 2 based on the language from the poem. Be prepared to defend your illustrations.

WEATHERS

Reflecting

F3

Debate whether or not one can experience positive
emotions if negative ones do not exist.

Monitoring and Assessing

F2

Draw a place that has meaning to you. Create at least 10 phrases that
provide imagery about your place. Read your phrases to a classmate
and ask him or her to recreate the scene. Compare your drawings.

Planning and Goal Setting

F1

How does Hardy use various literary elements (e.g., alliteration,
word repetition, punctuation) to create emotion?

WEATHERS

Sonnet 73
by William Shakespeare

That time of year thou mayst in me behold
When yellow leaves, or none, or few, do hang
Upon those boughs which shake against the cold,
Bare ruin'd choirs, where late the sweet birds sang.
In me thou seest the twilight of such day
As after sunset fadeth in the west,
Which by and by black night doth take away,
Death's second self, that seals up all in rest.
In me thou see'st the glowing of such fire
That on the ashes of his youth doth lie,
As the death-bed whereon it must expire
Consumed with that which it was nourish'd by.
This thou perceivest, which makes thy love more strong,
To love that well which thou must leave ere long.

Consequences and Implications

A3

What are the implications of the last two lines of the poem? What do the lines mean? Why didn't Shakespeare discuss love until the end?

Cause and Effect

A2

According to the poem, what effect does nearing the end of life have on Shakespeare?

Sequencing

A1

How does Shakespeare describe the sequence of life toward death?

SONNET 73

Generalizations

B3

What generalizations can be made about the use
of emotional language in the poem?

Classifications

B2

Categorize the words Shakespeare uses to evoke feeling.

Details

B1

What words in the poem does Shakespeare use to evoke feeling?

SONNET 73

Theme/Concept

C3

What does Shakespeare say about life? About love?

Inference

C2

What did Shakespeare mean by the phrase "As after sunset fadeth in the west, /Which by and by black night doth take away"?

Literary Elements

C1

Make a list of symbols and images in the poem and what they mean.

SONNET 73

The Clod and the Pebble

by William Blake

"Love seeketh not itself to please,
Nor for itself hath any care,
But for another gives its ease,
And builds a heaven in hell's despair."

So sung a little Clod of Clay,
Trodden with the cattle's feet,
But a Pebble of the brook
Warbled out these metres meet:

"Love seeketh only Self to please,
To bind another to its delight,
Joys in another's loss of ease,
And builds a hell in heaven's despite."

Generalizations

B3

What does Blake say about love in the poem? Write two generalizations.

Classifications

B2

How would you categorize the conflict or tension in the poem?

Details

B1

Based on the details you have read in this poem, would you say that Blake is satisfied or dissatisfied with love? Defend your position.

THE CLOD AND THE PEBBLE

Theme/Concept

C3

Create a new title for this poem. Explain why your title is meaningful.

Inference

C2

Compare and contrast the Clod and the Pebble.

Literary Elements

C1

How does this poem make you feel? Why? Use evidence from the text.

THE CLOD AND THE PEBBLE

Creative Synthesis

D3

Write a poem in the style of Blake's about a feeling, emotion, or characteristic (e.g., trust, greed, anger, love). Be prepared to share this poem.

Summarizing

D2

Summarize the main ideas in the poem.

Paraphrasing

D1

Draw a picture that paraphrases the intent of the poem.

THE CLOD AND THE PEBBLE

Name: _____ Date: _____

Hope Is the Thing With Feathers
by Emily Dickinson

Hope is the thing with feathers
That perches in the soul,
And sings the tune—without the words,
And never stops at all,
And sweetest in the gale is heard;
And sore must be the storm
That could abash the little bird
That kept so many warm.
I've heard it in the chillest land,
And on the strangest sea;
Yet, never, in extremity,
It asked a crumb of me.

Creative Synthesis

D3

Create a metaphorical poem à la Dickinson,
linking a living thing and a feeling.

Summarizing

D2

Summarize why Dickinson compares hope to a bird.

Paraphrasing

D1

Paraphrase the last two lines of the poem.

HOPE IS THE THING WITH FEATHERS

Using Emotion

E3

What advice would you give to Dickinson about hope? Why?

Expressing Emotion

E2

How do *you* cope with the demands of life?

Understanding Emotion

E1

How does Dickinson feel about the demands of life? Use evidence from the poem to support your response.

HOPE IS THE THING WITH FEATHERS

Name: _____   Date: _____

Stopping by Woods on a Snowy Evening

by Robert Frost

Whose woods these are I think I know.
His house is in the village though;
He will not see me stopping here
To watch his woods fill up with snow.

My little horse must think it queer
To stop without a farmhouse near
Between the woods and frozen lake
The darkest evening of the year.

He gives his harness bells a shake
To ask if there is some mistake.
The only other sound's the sweep
Of easy wind and downy flake.

The woods are lovely, dark and deep.
But I have promises to keep,
And miles to go before I sleep,
And miles to go before I sleep.

Name: _____ Date: _____

Consequences and Implications

A3

How do the punctuation, phrases, and rhythm of
this poem contribute to its meaning?

Cause and Effect

A2

What effect does the rhythm have on the overall mood of the poem?

Sequencing

A1

Notice the stanzas in the poem. Which ones are similar and different?
How might this be important to the meaning of the poem?

STOPPING BY WOODS ON A SNOWY EVENING

STOPPING BY WOODS ON A SNOWY EVENING

Generalizations

B3

What generalizations can you make about the conflicts in life, as expressed by Frost?

Classifications

B2

How would you categorize the conflict the man is facing?

Details

B1

What details in the poem are used to show conflict? Cite them.

Theme/Concept

C3

Is this poem more about beauty or regret? Which words and phrases in the poem support your answer?

Inference

C2

Why does Frost repeat the last two lines of the poem?

Literary Elements

C1

What is significant about the woods as the setting for this poem?

STOPPING BY WOODS ON A SNOWY EVENING

Name: _____   Date: _____

The Wild Swans at Coole
by William Butler Yeats

The trees are in their autumn beauty,
The woodland paths are dry,
Under the October twilight the water
Mirrors a still sky;
Upon the brimming water among the stones
Are nine-and-fifty Swans.

The nineteenth autumn has come upon me
Since I first made my count;
I saw, before I had well finished,
All suddenly mount
And scatter wheeling in great broken rings
Upon their clamorous wings.

I have looked upon those brilliant creatures,
And now my heart is sore.
All's changed since I, hearing at twilight,
The first time on this shore,
The bell-beat of their wings above my head,
Trod with a lighter tread.

Unwearied still, lover by lover,
They paddle in the cold
Companionable streams or climb the air;
Their hearts have not grown old;
Passion or conquest, wander where they will,
Attend upon them still.

But now they drift on the still water,
Mysterious, beautiful;
Among what rushes will they build,
By what lake's edge or pool
Delight men's eyes when I awake some day
To find they have flown away?

Generalizations

B3

What can you generalize about the author's
mood when writing this poem?

Classifications

B2

How would you categorize the mood of this poem? Why?

Details

B1

This poem evokes many feelings. How does this poem make
you feel? What details and phrases evoke specific feelings?

THE WILD SWANS AT COOLE

Theme/Concept

C3

Is this poem more about aging or lost love? Use evidence from the poem to support your answer.

Inference

C2

What is the significance of "nine and fifty Swans"? What phrases used later in the poem contribute to this significance?

Literary Elements

C1

Yeats uses symbolism to express deeper meaning in the poem. Make a list of symbols and their meanings. Be sure to include the following: autumn, swan, lake.

THE WILD SWANS AT COOLE

Creative Synthesis

D3

Some scholars have suggested that this poem is an autobiographical poem. Learn more about the life of William Butler Yeats. Create a memoir of Yeats and explain whether or not you believe this poem to be an autobiography.

Summarizing

D2

Summarize what Yeats meant by the last two lines of the poem.

Paraphrasing

D1

Paraphrase the second stanza of the poem.

THE WILD SWANS AT COOLE

Not They Who Soar
by Paul Laurence Dunbar

Not they who soar, but they who plod
Their rugged way, unhelped, to God
Are heroes; they who higher fare,
And, flying, fan the upper air,
Miss all the toil that hugs the sod.
'Tis they whose backs have felt the rod,
Whose feet have pressed the path unshod,
May smile upon defeated care,
Not they who soar.

High up there are no thorns to prod,
Nor boulder lurking 'neath the clod
To turn the keenness of the share,
For flight is ever free and rare;
But heroes they the soil who've trod,
Not they who soar!

Generalizations

B3

What generalizations does Dunbar make about slavery? Write at least two.

Classifications

B2

How does Dunbar categorize slaves and Blacks who are free?

Details

B1

List the ways in which Dunbar uses specific language to portray the differences between those who are free versus those who are slaves. What differences and similarities do you notice?

NOT THEY WHO SOAR

Theme/Concept

C3

How does Dunbar portray freedom and slavery?
Can one exist without the other?

Inference

C2

What is meant by "they who higher fare, /And, flying, fan
the upper air, /Miss all the toil that hugs the sod."?

Literary Elements

C1

Who are "they who soar"?

NOT THEY WHO SOAR

Creative Synthesis

D3

Create a new title that reflects Dunbar's intent for the poem.

Summarizing

D2

Find out more about Dunbar and the time period in which he wrote this poem. Summarize his life and the era in which he lived. How does his life story contribute to the overall meaning of the poem?

Paraphrasing

D1

Who are the heroes in the poem? How do you know?

NOT THEY WHO SOAR

Biographies

This chapter of *Jacob's Ladder* focuses on the use of biography as a specialized form of nonfiction in order to enhance students' understanding of their own career development and to teach metacognitive skills in the process. The use of Ladders E and F is evident in this section. Once students have completed the four biographies, additional analysis activities are included that encourage comparative analyses across the biographies.

The list of biographies with their ladders is found below:

Erwin Schrödinger
Physicist

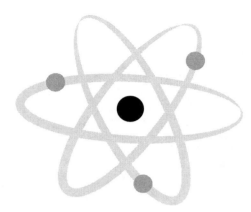

Considered to be one of the most important contributors to the field of theoretical physics, Erwin Schrödinger is celebrated today as a father of quantum mechanics, and the importance of his work is equated with that of Isaac Newton. Born in Vienna, Austria, in 1887, Schrödinger would go on to author six papers that explained the electron's movement as a wave, a conceptual breakthrough in quantum theory, and for which Schrödinger shared the Nobel Prize in Physics in 1933. In addition, he advanced the study of colorimetry (the study of human perception of color), joined his colleague Albert Einstein in the quest for a unified field theory, and lent his expertise to the most prestigious university faculties of the 20th century.

Schrödinger was born to Rudolf Schrödinger and Georgine Emilia Brenda. His father had studied chemistry, Italian painting, and botany, while his mother was the daughter of chemistry professor Alexander Bauer, who taught Mr. Schrödinger at university. Young Schrödinger was bilingual, speaking German and English, and was homeschooled for the first 10 years of his life. In 1898, he entered Akademisches Gymnasium, a renowned secondary school in Vienna, where he studied until 1906. Although he loved science, he was also fond of German poetry and studying ancient grammar. This multidisciplinary appreciation would follow him throughout his career. He was accepted to the University of Vienna in 1906, where he studied for 4 years under the illustrious physicist Friedrich Hasenöhrl, whose mentorship in the study of eigenvalue theories grounded Schrödinger's later work in quantum mechanics. Schrödinger was awarded his doctorate in 1910, and a year later he was offered an assistantship with another of his university professors, the famous physicist Franz Exner.

The year 1914 was marked by two important events for Schrödinger. He delivered his postdoctoral thesis, which was not unanimously embraced by the academic committee. Nevertheless, Schrödinger's first paper was published. More importantly, this year saw the beginning of WWI. Abandoning his academic posts temporarily, Schrödinger volunteered as an Austrian fortress artilleryman, and was sent to the Italian front. His mind was never far from his work, however, and he managed to publish from his post. In 1915, he was transferred to Hungary, where he continued to publish, and then again to Italy, where he was awarded a medal for outstanding service for his leadership in battle.

In 1917, Schrödinger returned to Vienna and taught a course in meteorology. It was at this time that he published his first paper on quantum theory. Additionally, he contributed to the theory of color vision, a subject to which he would devote much time in the next decade. Schrödinger became engaged to a young secretary, Anny Bertel, in 1919, and they were married in March the following year. His career took several turns in the early 1920s, as he traveled from Stuttgart, to Breslau, to Zurich, accepting positions at universities only to leave months later. During these transitions, he focused his work on colorimetry and published three papers on human color perception, which were inspired by the previous advances made by physicists Friedrich Kohlrausch, Hermann von Helmholtz, and Franz Exner. At Zurich, Schrödinger studied atomic structure and was colleagues with Hermann Weyl, a renowned mathematician who was both influential to Schrödinger's later work and a lover to Schrödinger's wife, Anny. Schrödinger himself had numerous love affairs, all of which Anny was aware, and he fathered three daughters by different women. His untraditional personal life was frowned upon by many of the universities where he worked, and, it is speculated, cost him faculty positions at various times in his life.

In 1924, Schrödinger became fascinated with the theories of Louis de Broglie, who introduced the concepts of wave-particle duality and the standing wave. Moreover, Schrödinger was neither satisfied with Niels Bohr's atomic model, which assumed a probabilistic nature of quantum physics; nor was he completely satisfied with the strictly mathematical formulation of quantum physics dominant at the time, Werner Heisenberg's theory of matrix mechanics. In 1926, Schrödinger published the first of six papers that would change the world of quantum physics irrevocably. In them, Schrödinger described several variations of an equation that described the movement of an electron as a wave, and which was named for him. His colleagues, including Albert Einstein, hailed Schrödinger's equation, and its variations, as the works of genius. In 1927, bolstered by his success, Schrödinger accepted a position at the University of Berlin, succeeding the great Max Planck.

Although he enjoyed the academically nurturing environment in Berlin, Schrödinger was alarmed by the rise of the Nazi party in Germany. He abhorred the group's anti-Semitic sentiments, and when, in 1933, the head of physics at the University of Oxford offered him a position, he fled Germany with several colleagues, publicly denouncing the Nazi party before he left. This statement of opposition would later haunt him when he returned to his native Austria. In the meantime, Schrödinger took with him to England his wife Anny and his colleague's wife Hilde March. Schrödinger fathered a child with Hilde, with whom Anny shared the responsibilities of motherhood.

Within the first week of his stay at Oxford, Schrödinger was notified that he had won the Nobel Prize in Physics for his work, which he was to share with fellow physicist Paul Dirac, who combined Schrödinger's equation and Heisenberg's matrix mechanics, proving that they described the same mathematical reality. Despite Schrödinger's achievement, the University of Oxford was uncomfortable with Schrödinger's family life and the fact that he essentially kept two wives, one of whom was married to another man. Tension surrounding this issue led to Schrödinger's leaving the university.

Soon after, Schrödinger made history again. In an informal correspondence with Einstein, Schrödinger proposed a thought experiment, which illustrated the conceptual problems he found in the probabilistic approach to quantum physics, often referred to as the Copenhagen Interpretation. This thought experiment was named the Schrödinger's Cat Paradox and was published in a paper entitled "The Present Situation in Quantum Mechanics." Schrödinger's conception of the paradox influenced thinkers for the next century and was the catalyst for much debate in the scientific community, inspiring others to write their own challenging variations of the experiment.

In 1936, after much private debate, Schrödinger accepted a position at the University of Graz in his native Austria. Despite the fact that Nazi Germany loomed at the Austrian border, Schrödinger longed to return to his birthplace. It was a decision that proved disastrous. When Germany annexed Austria in 1938, Schrödinger was immediately targeted as a political threat. The Nazis had not forgotten the physicist's criticisms made 5 years before as he fled Berlin. In a desperate effort to preserve his position at the university, and to remove the threat of Nazi retaliation, Schrödinger recanted his previous criticisms. He later apologized to his friend and colleague, Einstein, for this maneuver. It proved a useless strategy, and in 1939, he and Anny escaped to Italy.

A year later, Schrödinger was approached by the head of the Irish government, Éamon de Valera, who invited the physicist to be the Director for the School of Theoretical Physics in Dublin. Schrödinger accepted. For the next 17 years, he worked and lived in Dublin, delivering several series of well-attended, acclaimed lectures. In 1944, he published a book based on such a series, *What Is Life?*, in which he proposed the idea that the genetic code for life was housed in a complex sort of molecule. His work was not only derived from scientific first principles, but also by his philosophical beliefs. Early in his life, Schrödinger had discovered the work of German philosopher Arthur Schopenhauer. His metaphysical views galvanized a number of other scientists, including Einstein and Max Planck, and affected Schrödinger throughout his career. Moreover, Schopenhauer's philosophy shares some similarities to that of Vedanta Hinduism, another source of great creativity and illumination for Schrödinger. The publication of *What Is Life?* motivated Nobel Prize winner Francis Crick, who would later name the book as the inspiration for his discovery of the double helix structure for DNA.

During his years in Dublin, Schrödinger continued to publish. Many of his papers at that time explored the possibility of a unified field theory, one that would unify Einstein's theories of relativity and electromagnetism. He shared his desire for such a theory with his old friend Einstein, and the two corresponded enthusiastically about it until the mid-1940s. At that time,

Schrödinger prematurely and publicly announced a breakthrough in the theory, to which a dismayed Einstein responded with devastating criticism. The two broke off their correspondence in 1947, despite Schrödinger's attempts to apologize for his zealousness. Feeling that he was now too old to contribute great work to the field of theoretical physics, Schrödinger turned to his old passion, Greek history and philosophy. Work in this area of interest yielded a series of lectures, which were later transcribed into books entitled *Nature and the Greeks* and *Science and Humanism*. The lectures and the books were hailed as succinct and brilliant successes.

In 1955, Schrödinger retired, and a year later he left Dublin for his native Vienna. One year later, he was asked to give a lecture on nuclear energy at the World Energy Conference; however, he refused on the grounds that he did not believe it was possible. Instead, he gave a lecture on the philosophy of science. In later years, his interest in the unified field theory and general relativity continued, although he caused some controversy when he abandoned the traditional view of wave-particle duality, which relies on statistical approximations, in favor of a wave-only approach. He also published an autobiography begun 40 years previously, *Mein Leben, Meine Weltansicht*, which explored his metaphysical views and owed much to his lifelong study of Hinduism. Erwin Schrödinger died of tuberculosis in Vienna in 1961.

Consequences and Implications

A3

What are the positive and negative consequences
of being a leader in the scientific field?

Cause and Effect

A2

What were the effects of Schrödinger's failures on his success?

Sequencing

A1

Sequence the major accomplishments of Schrödinger's life.

ERWIN SCHRÖDINGER

Using Emotion

E3

Reflect upon a time in your life when you were heavily criticized. Write a journal entry about that time, including your thoughts and feelings about it. Include positive and negative outcomes of the criticism, both personally and academically.

Expressing Emotion

E2

When people are leaders in a field, they are more susceptible to criticism, as evidenced in Schrödinger's life. How do you respond when you are criticized? Is that response helpful or destructive to your overall success?

Understanding Emotion

E1

How do you think Schrödinger felt when others criticized his work? What is the evidence to support that view?

ERWIN SCHRÖDINGER

Reflecting

F3

What is success for you? Define it. How does that compare to society's definition? To Schrödinger's?

Monitoring and Assessing

F2

Successful events in life rarely happen by chance. They are a product of life-changing events and people, ability, hard work, and personality traits such as perseverance and resilience. Examine Schrödinger's successes. What positive and negative events and personality traits determined his success? What traits may have served to undermine him at certain stages? What about your successes? What events and personality traits make you successful? Unsuccessful?

Planning and Goal Setting

F1

Explain how Schrödinger achieved his successes. What was the role of interest, other people's ideas, and his own dogged determination in the process?

ERWIN SCHRÖDINGER

Margaret Bourke-White
Photographer

Margaret Bourke-White is best known as an intrepid photojournalist, who not only braved the perils of two wars, one helicopter crash, the violence of Partition in India, and being stranded in the Arctic, but also broke new ground for women in a field traditionally dominated by men. Born on June 14, 1904, in The Bronx, NY, Margaret was the daughter of second-generation immigrants Joseph White, an engineer for the printing industry and amateur inventor, and Minnie Bourke. Encouraged by her father, who took an interest in cameras, Margaret embraced photography as a hobby, but it wasn't until she started college that she began to see photography as a serious art form.

In 1922, Margaret began her studies at Columbia University, where she focused on herpetology. At the same time, her photography skills matured under the tutelage of the famous photographer Clarence White, who had recently opened a photography school in the city. However, after the devastating death of her father, Margaret withdrew from Columbia after only one semester. Two years later, she married her first husband, Everett Chapman, and after several transfers to different universities in the Midwest, she ultimately graduated from Cornell University. While at Cornell, Margaret's love for photography intensified. She captured Cornell's rural campus for the college newspaper, and upon graduation, determined to open her own photography studio in Ohio.

By 1927, Margaret had divorced Everett Chapman and was working as a leading industrial and architectural photographer in Ohio. Despite being a woman working in a predominately masculine career, the Otis Steel Company hired her to document the gritty, dangerous world of the steel mill worker. Her stunning photographs captured incredible scenes of hard labor, sparks, and molten flame, giving beauty to stark industrial scenes. These photographs caught the eye of the savvy publishing mogul Henry Luce, who was planning a magazine dedicated to celebrating American business and industry. He hired Margaret as the first female photojournalist for *Fortune* magazine in 1929, beginning a lifelong professional relationship that would help to define Margaret's career.

While working at *Fortune*, Margaret impressed critics and readers alike with her captivating photographs of modern industry. In 1930, she made history as the first Western photojournalist to be permitted into the Soviet

Union. There she documented the daily lives of Soviet citizens—their machinery, dams, and farms—giving American audiences their first, post-revolution glimpse of the Soviet Union. A collection of these photos, entitled Eyes on Russia, was published in 1931. Four years later, Margaret left *Fortune*, called upon by Henry Luce to be one of the first photojournalists for his new magazine, *Life*, a publication destined to become a household name in the years to come. Her photograph of Fort Peck Dam graced the first issue's cover in 1936, becoming a symbol of American potential and resilience in the dark days of the Great Depression. At this time, Margaret became a founding member of the American Artists' Congress, an organization dedicated to defending European artists against fascism, fighting against discrimination and the violation of civil liberties around the globe, and supporting the government's funding of the arts. While at *Life*, Margaret traveled to impoverished towns across the country, documenting the ravages of the Dust Bowl, and in 1937, she embarked on a journey to the American South, photographing the plight of poor tenant farmers.

It was during this time that she met her second husband, famous author Erskine Caldwell. Together, they produced the book *You Have Seen Their Faces,* which documented the social inequalities and impoverishment they witnessed across the Southern states. This publication represented Margaret's commitment to exposing social injustice through the lens of her camera. It was also the beginning of a creative partnership with Erskine Caldwell that continued until their divorce in 1942. They later saw the publication of their second work, *Say, Is This the U.S.A.,* which documented life in the United States before WWII.

In 1941, Margaret demonstrated her famous ability to be in the right place at the right time. She and Erskine were the only journalists in Moscow when Germany broke its peace agreement and invaded the Soviet Union. She delivered photographs of the horrible battle that ensued, and was soon shipped to Italy and Africa, where she was the first female war correspondent, but she was also the first female to be allowed into a combat zone in WWII. In 1945, she accompanied General Patton into Germany, and was one of the first photojournalists to document the atrocities of the Nazi prison camps. Her unflinching, devastating photographs of the Jewish survivors at Buchenwald gave American audiences a shocking glimpse of the brutal offenses committed by Nazi soldiers.

Following the war, she traveled to India, where she documented the terrible violence of Partition. Her famous photograph of Mohandas K. Gandhi reading a newspaper beside his spinning wheel was taken only hours before his assassination. From 1949 to 1953, she documented the lives of African mine workers under apartheid and captured images from the Korean War. Then, in the mid-1950s, she began to suffer from the early symptoms of Parkinson's disease. Two brain surgeries helped to control her tremors, but her speech was aversely affected. In 1963, her autobiography, *Portrait of Me,* was published, and became an instant bestseller.

Margaret Bourke-White died in Connecticut on August 27, 1971.

Generalizations

B3

Write three generalizations about factors that influence the lives of successful people.

Classifications

B2

Categorize those influences using at least three categories.

Details

B1

Outline the most important details and influences in Bourke-White's life.

MARGARET BOURKE-WHITE

Creative Synthesis

D3

You may have heard the saying, "A picture is worth a thousand words." Select one of Bourke-White's photographs and write a 3–4 page response to the photograph, based on how Bourke-White captured the event and what you imagine the picture is revealing.

Summarizing

D2

Find at least 10 photographs taken by Bourke-White. What features of Bourke-White's photos are distinctive? Summarize those features. Use specific examples.

Paraphrasing

D1

Explain the significance of Margaret-Bourke's gender in her role as a photographer.

MARGARET BOURKE-WHITE

Name: _____ Date: _____

MARGARET BOURKE-WHITE

Reflecting

F3

Write five ways you are successful and five things you need to work on to become more successful. Design a personal growth plan with realistic and achievable goals to become more successful in at least one area of your life.

Monitoring and Assessing

F2

What are you passionate about? How can you use that passion for success?

Planning and Goal Setting

F1

Passion and perseverance are two traits of successful individuals. Describe how this passion and perseverance were evidenced in Bourke-White's life.

Itzhak Perlman
Violinist

Regarded by many as the preeminent virtuoso violinist of his time, Itzhak Perlman astounds critics, audiences, and fellow musicians with his masterful technique, brilliant interpretations, and witty charm. His style, while technically superior and prodigiously executed, is accessible to all, endearing him to both erudite and popular audiences. Perlman's generosity of spirit is apparent in his dedication to the education of young musicians and his commitment to performing for global audiences. His is as equally adept at performing the entire classical repertoire as he is at jazz and klezmer. Consequently, Perlman has performed as a soloist in award-winning film scores.

Itzhak Perlman was born in August 1945, in Tel Aviv, the largest city in what was then Palestine. He was the son of Polish immigrant parents, Chaim and Shoshana Perlman. When he was 3 years old, young Perlman heard a concert of classical music on the radio, and was immediately transfixed. Wanting to develop his interest, Chaim, a barber, bought his son a used violin, which Perlman played daily. He continued to practice, without prompting, for the rest of his life.

It was only one year after the boy's fortuitous introduction to classical music that the Perlman family was struck with tragedy. At age 4, Perlman contracted polio. His life was spared, but his legs were paralyzed. As he gradually learned to walk again with the help of braces and crutches, he continued to play his violin, and he was soon given a scholarship to the Academy of Music in Tel Aviv. Studying under the famous Rivka Goldgart, it wasn't long before Perlman was nationally recognized as a prodigy. By 7 years of age, he was performing with the Ramat-Gan Orchestra in Tel Aviv and the Broadcasting Orchestra in Jerusalem. In 1955, he gave his first solo recital to a breathless Israeli audience, and his virtuosity claimed the ear of an American talent scout.

The talent scout was from the CBS network, and he invited Perlman to perform on *The Ed Sullivan Show*. In 1958, Perlman emigrated to the United States and performed Rimsky-Korsakov's "Flight of the Bumblebee" and Wieniawski's "Polonaise Brillante," for thousands of Americans. He was 13 years old. Soon after, he was awarded a scholarship to the distinguished Julliard School, where he finished his secondary education and studied under renowned violinists Ivan Galamian and Dorothy DeLay.

In 1963, Perlman made his debut at Carnegie Hall in New York, performing Wieniawski's Violin Concerto No. 1 in F-sharp minor. Although the concert was not well publicized, due to a newspaper strike, illustrious violinist Isaac Stern attended Perlman's incredible performance and promptly introduced the young violinist to his manager, Sol Hurok. In 1964, Perlman dazzled judges at the Leventritt Competition, a prestigious violin and piano competition. In a rare honor (the Leventritt Award is not often given), Perlman won the competition, which effectively launched his professional career. The following two years saw him touring as a soloist across the United States, performing in sold-out concerts. He made two more appearances on *The Ed Sullivan Show*, and traveled to Washington, DC, to perform Tchaikovsky's demanding Violin Concerto alongside the National Symphony Orchestra.

After this sensational performance, Perlman returned to Tel Aviv to play Tchaikovsky again, where he received a 15-minute standing ovation. That year, he played a season of concerts in Israel and made his British debut with the London Symphony Orchestra at Festival Hall. Another extensive tour in the United States culminated in a concert in Hawaii, where Perlman played the rarely performed Stravinsky's Violin Concerto. Stravinsky conducted.

In January 1967, Perlman paused in his incessant touring to marry fellow Julliard student, Toby Friedlander, whom he had met 3 years earlier at a summer camp concert. They would eventually settle in New York and raise five children together, as well as founding the Perlman Music Program in New York, a program dedicated to the education of gifted adolescent string players. Perlman continues his work in this program today, giving one-on-one lessons to students, many of whom receive scholarships to his program, just as he received scholarships for his musical education.

Soon after his marriage, Perlman began teaching master's classes with London's South Bank Summer Music Series, and in 1970, the violinist appeared on *Sesame Street* and *The Tonight Show*, proving his ability to engage both academic and popular audiences. Perlman accepted his first faculty position at the Conservatory of Music, Brooklyn College in 1975, and he returned that same year to Carnegie Hall, where he performed "Chiaroscuro" from Robert Mann's Duo for Violin and Piano, which was written specifically for Perlman.

In 1986, Perlman acquired the instrument he still uses today, the Soil Stradivarius, a violin made in 1714 by master luthier Antonio Stradivari. Previously owned by violin virtuoso Yehudi Menuhin, the Soil Stradivarius is known for its distinctive red varnish and superior sound. Later that year, President Ronald Reagan awarded Perlman the Medal of Liberty for his contributions to the United States.

Returning to Israel in 1987, Perlman joined the Israeli Philharmonic Orchestra and toured Eastern bloc countries, giving famous performances in Warsaw and Budapest. Three years later, he joined the Israeli Philharmonic again, touring the Soviet Union. An Emmy-award-winning PBS film, *Perlman in Russia*, documented the tour. Later that same year, Perlman performed with renowned cellist Yo-Yo Ma and others in Leningrad in celebration of Tchaikovsky's 150th birthday. In 1993, Perlman collaborated with John Williams and performed the solos in his score for Steven Spielberg's award-winning film *Schindler's List*. This was to be the first in a series of collaborations with the film composer. Perlman performed with Yo-Yo Ma on Williams' score for the film *Memoirs of a Geisha* in 2005, and the two reunited for President Barack Obama's inauguration ceremony, for which Williams composed a quartet, "Air and Simple Gifts."

Perlman was awarded his second national medal, the National Medal of Arts in 2000, by President Bill Clinton. A year later, he embarked in a new musical direction, adding the title of conductor to his list of accomplishments. From 2001 to 2005, he was the Principal Guest Conductor at the Detroit Symphony, and in 2002, he began a 2-year stint as the Music Advisor for the Saint Louis Symphony Orchestra. During this time, he succeeded his former instructor, Dorothy DeLay, as the Dorothy Richard Starling Foundation Chair in Violin Studies at Julliard, and in 2005, his alma mater awarded him an honorary doctorate at its 100th commencement ceremony. Perlman also holds honorary degrees from distinguished universities such as Harvard, Yale, and Brandeis, among others.

In 2007, Perlman was invited to perform at a State Dinner in honor of Queen Elizabeth II and His Royal Highness The Duke of Edinburgh. In the years that followed, the violinist expanded his role as conductor, leading performances by several international orchestras. In 2007, he was also appointed Principal Conductor for the Westchester Philharmonic.

Itzhak Perlman has performed with and conducted most of the prestigious orchestras in the world. He has won 15 Grammy awards, including a Lifetime Achievement Grammy in 2008, and four Emmy awards for documentary films. Now, at age 65, he remains dedicated to educating the next generation of violinists, as he continues to evoke awe in audiences and fellow musicians. A true genius who is satisfied only when he is challenged, Perlman is beloved worldwide.

ITZHAK PERLMAN

Creative Synthesis

D3

If you were to interview Perlman, what questions would you ask him? Why?

Summarizing

D2

From adversity comes triumph. Summarize how this is true in Perlman's life. Summarize how this is true in yours.

Paraphrasing

D1

In your own words, explain how polio affected Perlman's career.

Using Emotion

E3

Sometimes artists and musicians are very sensitive and emotional when creating music. Sometimes this emotion also makes them sensitive to others' comments or things around them. How do you think musicians balance their sensitivities? What do you do when you are emotional or you are in a group with someone who is more sensitive?

Expressing Emotion

E2

Listen to a recording of one of Perlman's performances. While you are listening, either draw or write whatever comes to mind as he plays. Explain your writing or drawing and how Perlman's piece is reflected in your creation.

Understanding Emotion

E1

How does music evoke emotion in you? Explain.

ITZHAK PERLMAN

Name: _____ Date: _____

Reflecting

F3

"A true genius who is satisfied only when he is challenged . . ." Why do you think the author concludes Perlman's biography in this way? Would you rather have a challenge and receive a poor grade or have an "easy A" without challenge? How does your attitude toward challenge contribute to your success?

Monitoring and Assessing

F2

Assess your current schedule. Write down what a typical day looks like for you. How do you think your time could be used more effectively and productively? Design a plan.

Planning and Goal Setting

F1

Even though Perlman was viewed as a natural talent, he still had to work hard and seek new challenges. How does hard work play a part in your life and achievement of goals?

ITZHAK PERLMAN

Amartya Sen
Economist

Amartya Sen is an eminent, Nobel Prize-winning economist and humanitarian renowned for his work in welfare economics. His theories on social choice have indelibly shaped economic policies worldwide and have awakened the minds of modern economists to the injustice and inequalities experienced by the poverty stricken, minorities, and women. He is often called "the Mother Theresa of economics," although he modestly eschews the title.

Sen was born into a family of academics on November 3, 1933. His birthplace was the college campus of Visva-Bharati in Santiniketan, West Bengal, India. The coeducational college, which was also a secondary school, was founded by Nobel Prize-winner and friend of the Sen family, Rabindranath Tagore. It was Tagore who gave Sen his first name, which means "immortality" in Sanskrit. Sen's grandfather, Kshiti Mohan Sen, taught Sanskrit and ancient Indian literature at the college, which was known for its commitment to progressive education. Sen's father, Ashutosh Sen, was a professor of chemistry at Dhaka University, located in what is now Bangladesh. His mother, Amita Sen, edited a literary magazine in Bengal.

As a young boy, Sen's parents moved from Dhaka to Bengal, where he attended classes at the Visva-Bharati school. There, he was encouraged to pursue a love of inquiry rather than good grades; in fact, academic competition was frowned upon by the teachers. Additionally, the school emphasized studies in diverse cultures, which did much to inspire admiration for pluralism in Sen. Ironically, this focus on tolerance and plurality was in stark contrast to the sectarian violence that had erupted in India in the 1940s. Citizens shunned their shared Indian identities in favor of strict identification with their different religious communities. Sen witnessed the violent consequences of this shift in identities when, as a teenager, he saw a Muslim day laborer stagger onto the family's property, bleeding profusely from multiple stab wounds. As Sen's father rushed the man, Kadar Mia, to the hospital, he explained that he had chosen, against his wife's advice, to accept work in a Hindu neighborhood because his family desperately needed the money. Upon learning that he was Muslim, a group of Hindus stabbed him in the street. The bleeding man died later at the hospital, and Sen was haunted with the implications of the poor man's story for the rest of his life. He concluded that poor economic conditions and social intolerance had left this man, and many more like him, vulnerable to injustice and violence. It was during this time that Sen also saw the ruination caused by the 1943 famine in Bengal, which would claim millions of lives. The fact that Sen's upper-middle-class family was unaffected, and only the poorest laborers went without food, would later inspire Sen's economic theories.

Upon graduating from Visva-Bharati, Sen moved to impoverished Calcutta, where he attended Presidency College and worked toward his

B.A. He majored in economics, minored in mathematics, and enjoyed the heated political debates he met with as an undergraduate. Although he was attracted to some of the beliefs espoused by the political left, he did not strongly identify with any particular political party. He embraced political tolerance, pluralism, and oppositional politics, which were values belittled by his left-leaning friends. It was a friend who first introduced Sen to the work of economist Kenneth Arrow, whose book *Social Choice and Individual Values*, published in 1951, proposed what is now known as Arrow's impossibility theorem, the idea that all majority rules, including the status quo, cannot yield truly democratic outcomes. His book focused mainly on voting choice. This landmark book was the catalyst for Sen's subsequent fascination with social choice theory, and Arrow's work would be the launching pad for Sen's later work.

In 1952, Sen was diagnosed with mouth cancer and underwent a harsh course of radiation at a time when people did not realize the perniciousness of such a treatment. He recovered, and in 1953, he graduated from Calcutta University and left for Trinity College at Cambridge University in England. At the time, the economists at Cambridge were embroiled in a contentious debate between those who followed Keynes' economic theories and those who favored the neoclassical approach. Sen identified with neither side, making him somewhat isolated in his interests. He was sheltered from the heat of this debate at Trinity College, where he studied under economists Maurice Dobb, Dennis Robertson, and Piero Sraffa, all of whom held different economic views but, nevertheless, got along together. Sen was attracted to the pluralism modeled in his college, and although he couldn't find anyone who embraced the social choice theories that fascinated him, he finished his dissertation and earned his B.A. in 1955. He promptly began work in his doctoral program at Cambridge.

As a doctoral student, Sen took a 2-year leave to travel to Calcutta, where he was supervised in his doctoral thesis by the great A. K. Dasgupta, an economic methodologist who was instrumental as Sen's mentor. Sen was offered the position of Professor of Economics at Jadavpur University. He accepted at the young age of 23. Upon finishing his thesis, he submitted it to be considered for the Prize Fellowship at Trinity College. He won the award, which allowed him to study anything he chose for 4 years. After receiving his doctorate in 1959, Sen spent the next 4 years studying philosophy at Cambridge. Sen's interest in philosophy complemented his interest in welfare economics, and he later wrote several papers in philosophy.

In 1960, Sen married his first wife, Nabaneeta Dev, whom he'd met while studying in India. They later had two daughters together, Nandana and Artara. For the next year, Sen escaped the still-broiling economic debates at Cambridge, and traveled to MIT and Stanford, where he was a visiting professor. Then, in 1963, he returned to India, where he taught economics at the University of Delhi. It was there that he began to truly immerse himself in his theories on social choice. Along with the well-respected applied economist K. N. Raj, he devoted himself to making the university a formidable school of economics. The pair had largely succeeded by the time Sen left India to accept a position at the prestigious London School of Economics, where he taught for 7 years.

In 1970, he published his remarkable work, *Collective Choice and Social Welfare*, which he had begun writing while still living in India. He was greatly aided in his endeavor by economists Kenneth Arrow and John Rawls, with whom he briefly taught a joint course at Harvard University. The book advanced the perspectives of welfare economics: that although governments should consider the best interest of the people, they should not concern themselves with defining perfect solutions to public welfare problems.

Within a year, Sen and his family relocated to England, where Sen was offered a faculty position at the prestigious London School of Economics. Although he was excited at the fresh intellectual opportunities the university offered, he suffered two major setbacks in his first years in England. First, his wife divorced him and returned to India. Second, Sen suddenly began experiencing alarming symptoms that suggested his mouth cancer had returned. Alarmed, Sen underwent exploratory surgery, during which doctors discovered that he suffered not from cancer, but from bone necrosis, due to the harmful course of radiation he'd received as an undergraduate in India.

Sen recovered after surgery, and went on to teach at the London School of Economics for the next 6 years. He met his second wife, Eva Colorni, who was an Italian economist. They later had two children. Eva encouraged Sen to consider practical work, extending the social choice theory to more applied problems. In this way, she offered great support to Sen, who felt she was a major influence on his work. In 1979, the fruits of this encouragement were born in a series of Tanner Lectures on Human Values, which Sen gave at Stanford University. These lectures were later compiled in a well-received essay, entitled "Equality of What." From 1977 to 1987, Sen served in two faculty positions at the Oxford University, and in 1981, he published the honored book *Poverty and Famines: An Essay on Entitlement and Deprivation*. In this masterwork, Sen examined famines that had occurred in Africa, China, and India, noting that starvation was not determined by an inadequate distribution of food, but rather by social factors (e.g., low wages, increased food costs, unemployment). He further explored the notion of positive freedom, which is defined as an individual's ability to take action. Positive freedom is dictated by an individual's capabilities, which might include opportunity, education, or health, to name a few. These capabilities ensure that an individual can enjoy positive freedom, a notion that was counter to that embraced by traditional economic theories. The book also recalled Sen's experiences in the Bengal famine of 1943. He noted that food supplies were actually more plentiful the year of the famine than they had been in previous nonfamine years. However, landless laborers were not paid enough to afford inflated food prices, which skyrocketed in response to British military and war costs. Thus, the most impoverished communities were those who starved, while middle- and upper class families were left unscathed.

The early 1980s were a productive time for Sen, who, with Eva's encouragement, published three more books: two collections of essays that reflected Sen's commitment to applying his theories to practical situations, *Choice, Welfare and Measurement* and *Resources, Values and Development*; and a book highlighting the role played by gender inequalities in starvation, *Commodities and Capabilities*. Although Sen received acclaim for these works, he also experienced tragedy. His wife Eva died suddenly in the early 1980s. Wanting a change of scene, Sen left England to accept a faculty position at Harvard University. He taught there from 1988 to 1998, during which time he published the essay "Gender and Cooperative Conflict," an empirical review of statistics concerning gender differences combined with comparative data Sen collected in the field. This was followed by another book, *Inequality Reexamined*, which further explored his capability approach to welfare economics. In 1998, Sen's contributions to the field of economics were awarded the highest honor, the Nobel Prize in Economic Science. In keeping with his devotion to equality and humanitarian aid, Sen used his prize money to establish the Pratichi Trust, which helps fund programs and works that fight against famine.

From 1998 to 2003, Sen was Master of Trinity College, the first Indian to fill this position. Following this post, he returned to Harvard University, where he currently sits as the Thomas W. Lamont University Professor of Economics. In addition to his Nobel Prize, Sen was also awarded the Bharat Ratna (Jewel of India), which is the highest honor awarded to a civilian for public service by the President of India. He is now remarried to economic historian Emma Georgina Rothschild, with whom he makes an annual sojourn to India. Beloved in his native country and around the world, Sen is widely considered to be the conscience of economics. He has dedicated his career to illuminating the plights of the impoverished and neglected populations across the globe, giving voice to millions whose suffering has been ignored by governments, academia, and their fellow countrymen.

Consequences and Implications

A3

What are the positive and negative consequences
of wealth, as shown by Sen's life?

Cause and Effect

A2

What effect did education and wealth have on Sen's life?

Sequencing

A1

Sequence the major events leading up to Sen's success.
Which events were most important to his future? Why?

AMARTYA SEN

Name: _____ Date: _____

Generalizations

B3

Write three generalizations about wealth. Link those generalizations to Sen's life and to your own.

Classifications

B2

Categorize your list.

Details

B1

Brainstorm as many things that you can think of that make people wealthy.

AMARTYA SEN

AMARTYA SEN

Using Emotion

E3

Should you give to homeless people? Why or why not? When does emotion need to be harnessed, and when is it good to make a difference in the world? Cite specific examples and ideas.

Expressing Emotion

E2

Think of a time when you were deeply moved by a person's story or event. What did you do? How did you react? How did you (or could you have) used your gifts and resources for the betterment of the situation or person?

Understanding Emotion

E1

How did Sen use his feelings about poverty for good?

Culminating Activities for Biographies

The following section has been created to provide additional challenge for gifted learners and their study of biography. These additional questions and activities are intended to provide connections across all of the biography studies read. These additional questions and activities may be used in discussion, as written work, or in centers during class time.

- Which of the four individual lives would you most like to emulate? Why?

- Examining only personality factors and the influence of significant people and events in the lives of these four individuals, who do you think was most successful and why?

- What internal and external motivators were present in the lives of all of these individuals? What do these patterns indicate about the lives of many successful individuals?

- How was the theme of overcoming adversity evidenced in the lives of each of these individuals? Why was this important to their success?

Select one of the following activities to complete.

Write your autobiography as if you were at the end of life, reflecting back. What significant events, experiences, and people heavily influenced your success from birth to where you are today? What challenges have you faced? What skills and personality traits do you need to develop next as you move to the next stage of life? How will you know if you are successful in your chosen career in 20 years? What criteria will you use to measure success?

Interview someone who has been influential in your life or someone you determine to be successful. To what does that person attribute his or her successes? Be sure to ask about personality traits, significant positive and negative events, influential people, and life circumstances that have shaped who this person is. Compare this person's patterns of success with the four individuals you have been studying.

Pre- and Postassessments and Exemplars

Appendix A contains the pre- and postassessment readings and answer forms, as well as a rubric for scoring the assessments. The preassessment should be administered before any work with *Jacob's Ladder* is conducted. After all readings and questions have been answered, the postassessment can be given to track student improvement on the ladder skill sets. Included in this appendix are example answers for both the pre- and postassessments. The answers are taken from student responses given during the piloting of this curriculum.

Name: _____ Date: _____

Pretest: Emily Dickinson Poem

Please read the poem by Emily Dickinson below. Answer the four questions related to the poem.

This is my letter to the world,
That never wrote to me,—
The simple news that Nature told,
With tender majesty.
Her message is committed
To hands I cannot see;
For love of her, sweet countrymen,
Judge tenderly of me!

1. What does the author think about the world? Provide evidence from the poem to defend your answer.

_____

_____

_____

_____

_____

2. What did the author mean when she wrote, "The simple news that Nature told, /With tender Majesty"? Provide evidence from the poem to defend your answer.

_____

_____

_____

_____

_____

3. What do you think this poem is about? Give a reason why you think so.

_____

_____

_____

_____

_____

_____

4. Create a title for this poem. Give a reason why your title is appropriate for this poem.

_____

_____

_____

_____

_____

_____

Posttest: Emily Dickinson Poem

Please read the poem by Emily Dickinson below. Then answer the four questions related to the poem.

> There is no frigate like a book
> To take us lands away,
> Nor any coursers like a page
> Of prancing poetry.
> This traverse may the poorest take
> Without oppress of toll;
> How frugal is the chariot
> That bears a human soul!

1. What does the author think about books? Provide evidence from the poem to defend your answer.

_____

_____

_____

_____

_____

_____

2. A frigate is a small warship. Why does the author compare a book to a frigate? Provide evidence from the poem to defend your answer.

_____

_____

_____

_____

_____

_____

3. What one word best describes what this poem is about? Give a reason why you think so.

_____

_____

_____

_____

_____

4. Create a title for this poem. Give a reason why your title is appropriate for this poem.

_____

_____

_____

_____

_____

Name: _____

Date: _____

Assessment Scoring Rubric

Question	Points				
	0	1	2	3	4
1 Implications and Consequences (Ladder A)	Provides no response or response is inappropriate to the task demand	Limited, vague, inaccurate; rewords the prompt or copies from text	Response is accurate and makes sense but does not adequately address all components of the question or provide rationale from text	Response is accurate; answers all parts of the question; provides a rationale that justifies answer	Response is well written, specific, insightful; answers all parts of the question, offers substantial support, and incorporates evidence from the text
2 Inference (Ladder C)	Provides no response or response is inappropriate to the task demand	Limited, vague, inaccurate; rewords the prompt or copies from text	Accurate response but literal interpretation with no support from the text	Interpretive response with limited support from the text	Insightful, interpretive, well-written response with substantial support from the text
3 Theme/ Generalization (Ladders B and C)	Provides no response or response is inappropriate to the task demand	Limited, vague, inaccurate; rewords the prompt or copies from text	Literal description of the story without explaining the theme; no reasons why	Valid, interpretive response with limited reasoning from the text	Insightful, interpretive response with substantial justification or reasoning
4 Creative Synthesis (Ladder D)	Provides no response or response is inappropriate to the task demand	Limited, vague, inaccurate; rewords the prompt or copies from text	Appropriate but literal title with no attempt to support	Interpretive title with limited reasoning or justification	Insightful, interpretive title with extensive justification or reasoning

Example Answers

Pretest: Emily Dickinson Poem

Note. These answers are based on student responses and teacher ratings from field trials conducted by the Center for Gifted Education and The College of William and Mary. The answers have not been changed from the original student responses.

1. **What does the author think about the world? Provide evidence from the poem to defend your answer.**

   1-point responses might include:

   - The author thinks the world can write.

   - The world doesn't like her.

   - She thinks that no one wrote her back.

   2-point responses might include:

   - I think the author feels good about the world and the way it looks.

   - I think the author thinks the world is graceful, beautiful, and majestic.

   - She loves the earth and everything on it.

   3-point responses might include:

   - She thinks the world is majestic because it says: "The simple news that nature told with tender majesty."

   - The author thinks the world is nice. I think this because she called the world (nature) tender (soft).

   4-point responses might include:

   - What the author thinks of the world is that nature sends a message. I know this because it says "The simple news that nature told."

   - The author thinks the world knows what she's like inside because it said in the poem "To hands I cannot see."

   - I think the author thinks the world is a place to be free because the author can express his or her feelings and write a "letter to the world."

2. **What did the author mean when she wrote "The simple news that Nature told, /With tender majesty"? Provide evidence from the poem to defend your answer.**

1-point responses might include:

- The author means that the world is filled with tender majesty.
- Nature told her thank you.
- Nature was happy.

2-point responses might include:

- I think the author meant that nature was trying to tell her something.
- The author meant that nature tells a story softly and gently.
- She means that people should treat the forests with care.

3-point responses might include:

- I think the author meant that nature told the author a kind message, because tender means kind.
- The author meant that nature was answering her letter and sharing news. She meant that nature was beautiful because if something is majestic that usually means it is beautiful.
- I think she meant the world was good because tender majesty makes me think of a "soft world."

4-point responses might include:

- The author meant that Nature's news was weather because "The simple news" is the rain and snow. Weather can be tender, like soft snow.
- I think it means that nature has shared news with the author. Nature can't speak or write therefore nature has never written to the author but given her news in other ways.
- I think "The simple news that Nature told with tender majesty" means nature is sharing sad news. Because the line "her message is committed" makes the news seem important and the line "for love of her sweet countrymen" sounds like the news is sad.

3. **What do you think this poem is about? Give a reason why you think so.**

1-point responses might include:

- I think this poem is about what the author thinks about the world.

- It's about sending a letter to the world.

- Nature, that's what it talks about the most.

2-point responses might include:

- I think this poem is about how much the author loves the world because she is talking about how beautiful the world is.

- It is about the world because it talks about nature.

- I think this poem is about nature and its message.

3-point responses might include:

- I think it is about how nature relies on people.

- I think it is about the freedom to say what you think.

- This poem is about Mother Nature and the story she tells.

4-point responses might include:

- I think this poem is about a girl who wants to know what the world thinks of her because at the end of the poem she says "Judge tenderly of me."

- I think this poem is about a relative who past away because it said "to hands I can not see." The news that nature told is sad news of a death.

- This poem is about telling the world about pollution but no one will listen. "The simple news nature told me" is Mother Nature is being polluted and so the author is telling the world to stop.

4. **Create a title for this poem. Give a reason why your title is appropriate for this poem.**

1-point responses might include:

- World

- Here's a Letter because the poem is a letter.

- To: World From: Me

2-point responses might include:

- I think The World would be a good title because the whole poem talks about the world.

- My Letter to the World would be a good title because the poem is about some-one writing a letter to the world.

- The title should be Nature because the whole poem is about nature.

3-point responses might include:

- The Poem of Love, because it is a touching and sweet poem.

- Majestic World is a good title because one of the lines says "The simple news that nature told, with tender majesty." So this line shows that the author thinks the world is majestic.

- Nature's Message would be a good title because the author talks about nature "talking" to her.

4-point responses might include:

- My title is World Peace. I think it's a good title because the author tells about how tender and sweet the world is. The author says "For love of her" showing that people should protect the world.

- I would name this poem The Message that Never Got Sent because it sounds like the author is trying to tell the world a message about nature but no one is listening.

- The World Should Know. I think this would be a good title because the poem is a letter about what the author thinks is important. The author wants to share what she knows about nature.

Example Answers

Posttest: Emily Dickinson Poem

Note. These answers are based on student responses and teacher ratings from field trials conducted by the Center for Gifted Education at The College of William and Mary. The answers have not been changed from the original student responses.

1. **What does the author think about books? Provide evidence from the poem to defend your answer.**

   1-point responses might include:

   - The author thinks there is no frigate like a book. This evidence is in the first sentence first paragraph.
   - She thinks that books are a frigate which might mean warship.
   - The author thinks books are fun and good.

   2-point responses might include:

   - The author thinks books are like nothing else. I think that because the author says books are not like frigates or courses.
   - She thinks highly of books because she said "There is no frigate like a book" which means that she likes books a whole lot.
   - I think the author likes books because she compared a lot of things to them.

   3-point responses might include:

   - She thinks books are just like frigates because they take you lands away.
   - The author loves books. I know this because during the poem she talks about how books can give you stories you can think up in your imagination.
   - The author thinks that books take you to different places and are good because she says "There is no frigate like a book" and "Nor courses like a page."

   4-point responses might include:

   - Emily Dickinson thinks books are a good way of learning and there are many places to borrow them, like a library where you don't have to pay. I know this because she said "This traverse may the poorest take without oppress of toll."
   - I think the author likes books and really gets into them because she said "there is no frigate like a book to take us lands away." Also, I think she believes every page counts and that they can take you dashing through the story or poem because she said "nor any courses like a page of prancing poetry."

- The author thinks that books can take your mind to distant places without ever leaving your home. I think this because of the sentence from the author's poem: "There is no frigate like a book to take us lands away."

2. **A frigate is a small warship. Why does the author compare a book to a frigate? Provide evidence from the poem to defend your answer.**

   1-point responses might include:

   - Some books have warships in them.

   - They are two things you can see.

   - She is comparing a frigate to a book. She said that there is no frigate like a book.

   2-point responses might include:

   - The author is comparing a book to a frigate because she thinks they are the same.

   - She compares a frigate to a book because to her a book is a small warship.

   - The author compares a book to a warship because she likes books as much as a small warship.

   3-point responses might include:

   - She compares the two because when she says "To take us lands away," she means that a book is like a warship. A ship is a form of transportation and a book can make your mind think about the place you are reading about.

   - I think the author compared a book to a frigate because she said a book goes to far lands and a frigate travels to lands far away.

   - The author compares a book to a frigate because they both bear a human's soul.

   4-point responses might include:

   - The author compares a frigate to a book because a frigate is small so it can deliver soldiers to far away places and a book can take our imaginations to far away places.

   - I think she is trying to say that a book can be powerful, even more powerful than a warship. In the poem she says "There is no frigate like a book to take us lands away, Nor any course like a page."

   - She compares a book to a frigate because you can travel to say, Antarctica, just by opening a book. A frigate can also take you to different countries, but it might take hours.

3. **What one word best describes what this poem is about? Give a reason why you think so.**

   1-point responses might include:

   - Frigate
   - Like
   - Neat, because it talks about warships and she uses big and new words.

   2-point responses might include:

   - Books, because she pretty much talks just about books in her story.
   - War! This one word describes the poem because the poem said there is "no frigate like a book."
   - The word I pick is amazing because it is so powerful.

   3-point responses might include:

   - Books, because the author explains why she loves books so much and tells what happens when she reads different kinds of book. She tells what happens in her imagination.
   - Joy would be the one word that best describes what this poem is about. I chose that word because the poem says that books and poetry are really good.
   - Read, I think that because she promotes reading throughout the entire poem.

   4-point responses might include:

   - The one word that best describes what the poem is about is imaginative. I think this because she thinks books take you to mystic places.
   - Relaxing, I chose relaxing because when you read this poem it makes you want to grab a book and get comfortable.
   - Magic, I think that the poem is about the magic of reading. I think that because it talks about where a book can take you.

4. **Create a title for this poem. Give a reason why your title is appropriate for this poem.**

   1-point responses might include:

   - A book.
   - Books and Warships
   - A Poem about Books

2-point responses might include:

- I think a good title for this story might be War because it talks about warships.

- A book because it talks about books.

- Frigate. This is a good name for it because he talks about a frigate.

3-point responses might include:

- I think a good title for this poem is Books because it compares books to other things.

- Read to Find is the title I would pick. I think this because you find out things when you read.

- Read a Book. This title says a lot about the poem, because the author encourages you to read in this poem.

4-point responses might include:

- The Magic of Words. I think it is good because the poem talks about books being magical, taking you to magical places.

- I think The Joy of Reading would be a good title because she talks about enjoying reading in this poem.

- A good title would be All Around the World with a Book. I think this because the poem talks about the many places around the world you can go by reading.

Student Product Task Demand

(Postassessment Only)

Ask students to create an original written piece (it may be a story, a fable, or a poem) that expresses a specific theme of their choosing (e.g., loyalty, redemption, courage). They may use any of the readings in *Jacob's Ladder* as a model for their work. The original piece must tell a story using a main character, a conflict, and a resolution. The selection should focus on providing an engaging plot with appropriate use of structure, detail, images, and symbols. The selection should not exceed 1,000 words. The student should spend one hour planning the piece (e.g., outlining, doing prewriting, doodling, illustrating), 2 hours drafting the piece, one hour proofing and revising, and one hour answering the questions posed below.

Once the piece has been written, proofread, and edited by the student, the following questions should be answered on another piece of paper:

My piece is a _____ (identify genre here) and was modeled after _____ (identify author and title of selection here).

1. What concept did I try to manipulate in my written piece? Why did I choose this concept?

2. What were the story elements that I included (e.g., character, plot, setting, theme)? How did I plan for them? In what order?

3. What images and symbols were used? Why are they significant?

4. What features make my plot engaging?

5. How did I assess my piece critically? What criteria did I apply to judge its effectiveness?

6. As I use the attached rubric to judge my piece, what areas for improvement might I apply to new work? What aspects of the piece did I execute well?

Name: _____   Date: _____

Rubric for Creative Writing

The following items should be assessed, using a 1–4 scale, with 1 being highly ineffective, 2 being ineffective, 3 being effective, and 4 being highly effective. Any item may also receive an N/A, meaning that the criterion was not addressed.

Criteria	Highly Ineffective	Ineffective	Effective	Highly Effective	N/A
The student has organized the piece according to the creative writing model provided.	1	2	3	4	N/A
The student has modeled the elements of a given writing genre in the piece (e.g., poetry, short story, fable).	1	2	3	4	N/A
The student has used an appropriate concept in a complex way.	1	2	3	4	N/A
The student has demonstrated an understanding of how to engage the reader into the plot without making the concept obvious.	1	2	3	4	N/A
The student applies appropriate metacognitive skills to critique work.	1	2	3	4	N/A
The student has included symbols, images, metaphors, or similes to illustrate ideas.	1	2	3	4	N/A

Rubric for Creative Writing, *continued*

What are the major strengths of the written selection?

What are the areas for improvement?

What further readings might enhance student understanding of the creative writing process?

What evidence is provided that the student can use a major concept and story elements to express ideas effectively?

What evidence is provided that the student has developed metacognitive skills of planning, writing, and reflecting?

APPENDIX

B

Record-Keeping Forms/ Documents

Appendix B contains three record-keeping forms and documents:

1. *Brainstorming/Answer Sheet*: This should be given to students for completion after reading a selection so that they may jot down ideas about the selection and questions prior to the discussion. The purpose of this sheet is to capture students' thoughts and ideas generated by reading the text. This sheet should act as a guide when students participate in group or class discussion.

2. *My Reflection on Today's Reading and Discussion*: This form may be completed by the student after a group or class discussion on the readings. The reflection page is designed as a metacognitive approach to help students reflect on their strengths and weaknesses and to promote process skills. After discussion, students use the reflection page to record new ideas that were generated by others' comments and ideas.

3. *Classroom Diagnostic Form*: These forms are for teachers and are designed to aid them in keeping track of the progress and skill mastery of their students. With these charts, teachers can look at student progress in relation to each ladder skill within a genre and select additional ladders and story selections based on student needs.

Name: _____ Date: _____

Brainstorming/Answer Sheet

Use this form to brainstorm thoughts and ideas about the readings and ladder questions before discussing with a partner.

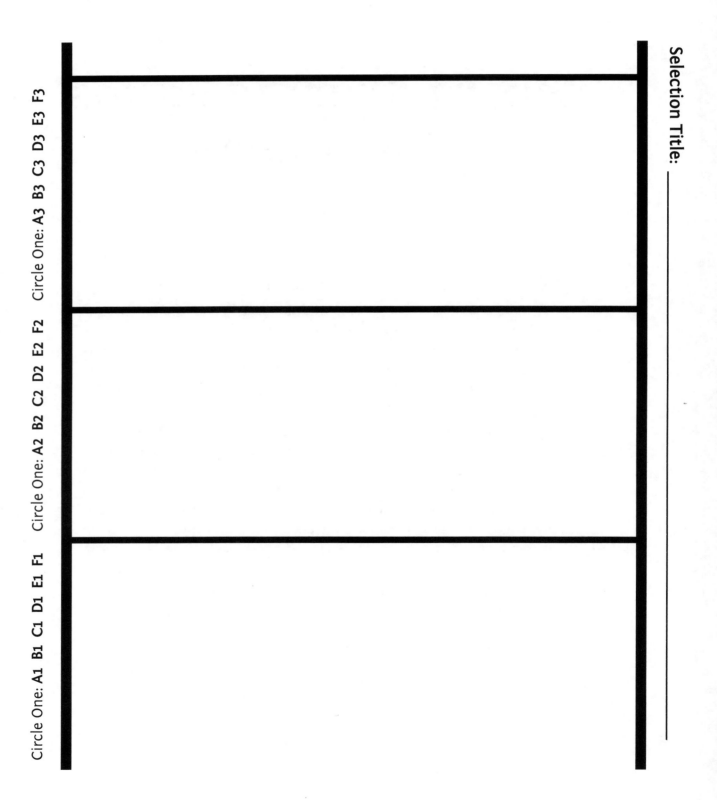

Circle One: **A3 B3 C3 D3 E3 F3**

Circle One: **A2 B2 C2 D2 E2 F2**

Circle One: **A1 B1 C1 D1 E1 F1**

Selection Title: _____

Name: _____ Date: _____

My Reflection on
Today's Reading and Discussion

Selection Title: _____

What I did well:

_____

_____

_____

_____

What I learned:

_____

_____

_____

_____

New ideas I have after discussion:

_____

_____

_____

_____

Next time I need to:

_____

_____

_____

_____

Classroom Diagnostic Form

Short Stories

Use this document to record student completion of ladder sets with the assessment of work.

0 = Needs Improvement   1 = Satisfactory   2 = Exceeds Expectations

Student Name	The Wolf and the Kid		The Last Lesson			The Mouse			The Ransom of Red Chief			The Monkey's Paw			The Diamond Necklace			The Celebrated Jumping Frog of Calaveras County			The Lottery Ticket		
	D	E	A	C	F	A	C	E	C	D	E	A	B	D	A	C	E	A	C	D	B	C	E

Jacob's Ladder Reading Comprehension Program, Level 4 © Prufrock Press • This page may be photocopied or reproduced with permission for single classroom use.

Classroom Diagnostic Form
Poetry

Use this document to record student completion of ladder sets with the assessment of work.

0 = Needs Improvement   1 = Satisfactory   2 = Exceeds Expectations

Student Name	Weathers			Sonnet 73			The Clod and the Pebble			Hope Is the Thing With Feathers			Stopping by Woods on a Snowy Evening			The Wild Swans at Coole			Not They Who Soar		
	A	D	F	A	B	C	B	C	D	D	E	A	B	C	B	C	D	B	C	D

Classroom Diagnostic Form

Biographies

Use this document to record student completion of ladder sets with the assessment of work.

0 = Needs Improvement   1 = Satisfactory   2 = Exceeds Expectations

Student Name	Erwin Schrödinger			Margaret Bourke-White			Itzhak Perlman			Amartya Sen		
	A	E	F	B	D	F	D	E	F	A	B	E

Jacob's Ladder Reading Comprehension Program, Level 4 © Prufrock Press • This page may be photocopied or reproduced with permission for single classroom use.

Alignment to Standards

Appendix C provides teachers with a guide to the content and themes within the readings. For each selection, a chart delineates the national standards addressed by the readings.

Standards Alignment

Short Stories

Language Arts: Short Stories	The Wolf and The Kid	The Last Lesson	The Mouse	The Ransom of Red Chief	The Monkey's Paw	The Diamond Necklace	The Celebrated Jumping Frog of Calaveras County	The Lottery Ticket
The student will use analysis of text, including the interaction of the text with reader's feelings and attitudes to create response.	X	X	X	X	X	X	X	X
The student will interpret and analyze the meaning of literary works from diverse cultures and authors by applying different critical lenses and analytic techniques.	X			X				X
The student will use knowledge of the purposes, structures, and elements of writing to analyze and interpret various types of text.	X	X	X	X	X	X	X	X
The student will use word-analysis skills, context clues, and other strategies to read fiction and nonfiction with fluency and accuracy.	X	X	X	X	X	X	X	X

Standards Alignment

Poetry

Language Arts: Poetry	Weathers	Sonnet 73	The Clod and the Pebble	Hope is the Thing With Feathers	Stopping by Woods on a Snowy Evening	The Wild Swans at Coole	Not They Who Soar
The student will use analysis of text, including the interaction of the text with the reader's feelings and attitudes, to create response.	X	X	X	X	X	X	X
The student will interpret and analyze the meaning of literary works from diverse cultures and authors by applying different critical lenses and analytic techniques.	X						X
The student will use knowledge of the purposes, structures, and elements of writing to analyze and interpret various types of text.	X	X	X	X	X	X	X
The student will use word-analysis skills, context clues, and other strategies to read fiction and nonfiction with fluency and accuracy.	X	X	X	X	X	X	X

Standards Alignment

Biographies

Social Studies and Science Standards	Erwin Schrödinger	Margaret Bourke-White	Itzhak Perlman	Amartya Sen
Social Studies Standards				
Culture	X	X	X	X
People, Places, and Environments	X	X	X	X
Individual Development and Identity	X	X	X	X
Individuals, Groups, and Institutions	X			X
Science Standards				
Science in Personal and Social Perspectives	X			
History and Nature of Science	X			

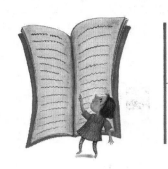

About the Authors

Tamra Stambaugh is a research assistant professor of special education and director of Programs for Talented Youth at Vanderbilt University. She is the coauthor of *Comprehensive Curriculum for Gifted Learners* and co-editor of *Overlooked Gems: A National Perspective on Low-Income Promising Students*, the *Jacob's Ladder Reading Comprehension Program* (both with Joyce VanTassel-Baska) and *Leading Change in Gifted Education* (with Bronwyn MacFarlane). Stambaugh has also authored or coauthored journal articles and book chapters on a variety of topics focusing on curriculum, instruction, and leadership. Her current research interests include the impact of accelerated curriculum on student achievement, teacher effectiveness, and talent development factors—especially for students of poverty.

Dr. Stambaugh serves as a member of the National Association for Gifted Children's professional standards committee and the Higher Education workgroup. She is the recipient of several awards, including the Margaret The Lady Thatcher Medallion for scholarship, service, and character from The College of William and Mary School of Education. Prior to her appointment at Vanderbilt, she was director of grants and special projects at The College of William and Mary, Center for Gifted Education, where she also received her Ph.D. in educational planning, policy, and leadership with an emphasis in gifted education and supervision.

Joyce VanTassel-Baska is the Jody and Layton Smith Professor Emerita of Education and former Executive Director of the Center for Gifted

Education at The College of William and Mary in Virginia, where she developed a graduate program and a research and development center in gifted education. She also initiated and directed the Center for Talent Development at Northwestern University. Prior to her work in higher education, Dr. VanTassel-Baska served as the state director of gifted programs for Illinois, as a regional director of a gifted service center in the Chicago area, as coordinator of gifted programs for the Toledo, OH, public school system, and as a teacher of gifted high school students in English and Latin. She is past president of The Association for the Gifted of the Council for Exceptional Children, the Northwestern University Chapter of Phi Delta Kappa, and the National Association for Gifted Children.

Dr. VanTassel-Baska has published widely, including 27 books and more than 500 refereed journal articles, book chapters, and scholarly reports. Recent books include: *Content-Based Curriculum for Gifted Learners* (2011, with Catherine Little), *Patterns and Profiles of Low-Income Learners* (2010), and *Social and Emotional Curriculum With Gifted and Talented Students* (2009, with Tracy Cross and Rick Olenchak). She also served as the editor of *Gifted and Talented International,* a publication of the World Council on Gifted and Talented, for 7 years from 1998–2005.